The Seven Deadly Stupidities

Using Other People's Failures to Make Better Decisions

Written by
George Pillari

Foreword by
Guy Kawasaki

RUNNING FOX PARTNERS

ISBN: 979-8-9910128-0-5

Library of Congress Control Number: 2024912674

Printed in the United States of America

For dad. You would have disagreed with much of what is here, but you still would have been proud.

Table of Contents

Foreword

We've all made stupid mistakes. I know I have. Yet, we tend to glorify success and sweep failure under the rug. My friend, George Pillari, wants to change that. In *The Seven Deadly Stupidities*, he argues convincingly that we can learn as much from others' dumb mistakes as their victories.

This book is a master class in avoiding catastrophe. It exposes cringeworthy blunders across business, politics, sports and more, like when J.P. Morgan acquired Frank Financial Aid for $175 million without realizing 90 percent of its customer database was fake, or when the captain of cargo ship *El Faro* sailed into a hurricane based on six-hour-old weather data rather than current forecasts. Don't even get me started on WeWork burning $200 million per month because its business model was built on quicksand.

Yet, the book also shows how smart people make dumb decisions all the time. Overconfidence and ego frequently override logic and data. FOMO drives lemming-like behavior. Quick fixes create bigger problems later. Even the best and brightest make totally avoidable screwups.

If you read nothing else, check out the story of Soviet officer Stanislav Petrov. His clear-headed decisions in 1983 literally prevented nuclear Armageddon and saved humanity. One man overcame emotion, bias, and protocol to make the right call when the stakes were ultimate. We should all aspire to that level of composure under pressure.

The Seven Deadly Stupidities is a must-read for any leader or decision-maker. Learn from the blunders of others so you can avoid catastrophe and maximize success.

As George likes to say, 80 percent of success is simply not being stupid. This book shows you how to avoid stupid mistakes and even be remarkable.

Guy Kawasaki
Chief Evangelist of Canva and Author of *Think Remarkable*

Introduction

*It's good to learn from your mistakes. It's better to
learn from other people's mistakes.*
~ Warren Buffett

History repeats itself. Unfortunately, so does bad
decision-making. The thesis of this book is if you can
avoid the seven deadly stupidities, you can learn
from the failures of others and make better
decisions.

A few years ago, I got sick of it. Every airport
bookstore was selling the same business books.
Every business book promised how to help you
boost your career, form better habits, become a
great communicator, and dozens of other cliches.
Funny thing is people bought millions of these
books. I guess we all want a step-by-step approach
to the inevitable positive outcome, since that seems
to be what all these books have been telling us.

The inherent problem is that many things do
not work. If all those books (and their TED-talking
authors) were right, there would be about a billion
surplus CEOs and nobody left to do the work.

Earlier in my career, I came to the realization
that failure is far more prevalent than success.
Achieving success was less about how great the

product was and more about convincing people that you were not going to fail or be crushed by a competitor.

Consider a few numbers that frame this issue: In a typical year, there are about 350 IPOs, or Initial Public Offerings, of companies. (An IPO is a concrete marker of success.) In that same typical year, there are more than 10,000 corporate bankruptcies.

Need I say more?

This book is the result of my experiences and observations as an entrepreneur, public-company CEO, crisis-manager, and father of five. The key takeaway from this work is that rather than chase an ideal of success, we should learn from the failures of others and avoid those failures ourselves.

To succeed, you do not need to be the smartest or the most cunning, but if you are aware of and account for the stupidities of others, you will have a much better chance of success.

Why use "stupidities" in the title and as a theme throughout the book? Simple, we are all stupid at some point. Personally, I have lived through all seven of the stupidities we will discuss in this book – and have the bruises to prove it.

There is an old saying, "80 percent of success is showing up." Well, my twist on this is, "80 percent of success is avoiding stupidity." It is less common to consider what needs to be eliminated, not added, for success to be more probable.

Rather than write an autobiographical book about all the times I was stupid, I selected case studies from my readings and experiences over the years. Some of the stories were high-profile failures while others were more subtle.

How to Read This Book

This book is divided into eight sections, with one for each of the seven deadly stupidities and a final section to show you how to put it all together and avoid stupidity. Within each section are chapters to illustrate each stupidity from multiple perspectives. Within each chapter, a case study is included to demonstrate how each stupidity resulted in failure instead of success.

- *Section 1 (Chapters 1-6): Going for the Moonshot* begins with the story of Thomas Edison and poses the question, was he a great inventor or really a great businessperson? In Chapter 2, Google X called itself the Moonshot Factory, but was it really? What about the different approach taken by the man in the moonshot, Elon

Musk with SpaceX? You will learn more about this in Chapter 3. In Chapter 4, the ill-fated moonshot of Lance Armstrong is explored. And in Chapter 5, you will learn that the invention of the World Web was the accidental moonshot of academic scientist Tim Berners-Lee. Chapter 6 will sum up the stupidity of a going for the moonshot and how to avoid it.

- *Section 2 (Chapters 7-10): Surrendering to FOMO* includes the stories of the young and telegenic Elizabeth Holmes and the Theranos house of cards, followed by Chapter 8 and the failure of Webvan, the first online grocery store, which was backed by elite venture capitalists who impulsively continued to throw money at the company, despite Webvan's inability to prove its business in its first market. In Chapter 9, you will meet Sam Bankman-Fried, the Pied Piper of crypto, who led his followers down the drain and himself into prison. Chapter 10 will sum up the stupidity of surrendering to FOMO and how to avoid it.

- *Section 3 (Chapters 11-12): Relying On Family and Friends* pits TigerMom against RationalMom in Chapter 11 and their diametrically opposed views of how to help a child prepare for and make a college selection. It's a clash of parenting ideologies. Chapter 12 will sum up the stupidity of relying on family and friends and how to avoid it.

- *Section 4 (Chapters 13-16): Getting Blinded by the Upside* tells three different stories. In Chapter 13, you will learn about the preventable sinking of the 792-foot cargo ship *El Faro* and, in Chapter 14, the demise of former McKinsey & Co. chairman Raj Gupta. Both felt the full force of being blinded while, in Chapter 15, Alabama football coach Nick Saban had no choice but to go for the upside. Chapter 16 will sum up the stupidity of getting blinded by the upside and how to avoid it.

- *Section 5 (Chapters 17–20): Trusting the Media* gets more difficult when we learn in Chapter 17 about reporters who worked for the CIA and, in Chapter 18, former military officials, generals-turned-analysts, who went on television while secretly being on the payroll of the Pentagon. In Chapter 19, James Frey, author of *A Million Little Pieces,* exemplifies the misplaced value society puts on celebrity journalists, even when they lie. Chapter 20 will sum up the stupidity of trusting the media and how to avoid it.

- *Section 6 (Chapters 21-25): Using Quick and Dirty Thinking* introduces us in Chapter 21 to the misuse of rules of thumb, bias, and heuristics, the Black Death of decision-making. With bias, we allow activities controlled by impulses to seep into the orderly process of our logical thinking. In Chapter 22, you will meet Rosalie Bradford, who lost 900 pounds, and Roger Bannister, who was a medical student who -- with little time to train -- was the first person in history to break the four-minute mark in the one-mile run. In Chapter 23, you will discover that preparing for a job interview is not a place for quick and dirty thinking and, in Chapter 24, neither was the planning that led to the catastrophic implosion of the Titan submersible. Chapter 25 will sum up the stupidity of using quick and dirty thinking and how to avoid it.

- *Section 7 (Chapters 26-31): Neglecting to Measure Twice* introduces us in Chapter 26 to Charlie Javice, the twenty-something founder of Frank Financial, who scammed J.P. Morgan out of $175 million and, in Chapter 27, to Jeff Skilling, former president of Enron, whose creative accounting cost shareholders billions. In Chapter 28, Adam Neumann and his charade called WeWork makes an appearance and in Chapter 29 we hear about Gawker Media, which was slaughtered by billionaire Peter Thiel for privacy violations. In Chapter 30, you will learn that one of the most successful companies ever, Starbucks, did measure twice. Chapter 31 will sum up the stupidity of neglecting to measure twice and how to avoid it.

- *Section 8 (Chapter 32): Putting It All Together* tells the story of Soviet General Stanislav Petrov, who stared down all seven of these stupidities and prevented a global thermonuclear war.

The book concludes with a look at some of the stupidity-defying heroes. Yes, some people got it right.

I have always enjoyed books written by journalists because the chapters were short. I could read them for fifteen minutes, put the book down, and pick it up again a few days later. This is the style of *The Seven Deadly Stupidities*. You can read a section at a time (e.g., all the chapters in the section on Surrendering to FOMO) or you can skip around and read a chapter or two from any section, especially if you are familiar with a particular case study.

I recommend reading *Section 8: Putting It All Together* as your last section, since it references many of the stories shared in the book.

Let's get started with learning from the failures of others so you can eliminate stupidity and make better decisions.

Decisions About Decisions

In the psychology literature, there are many references to the fact that we make 35,000 decisions per day, of which about seventy are real decisions that are made consciously. Some of these include what to wear, what to eat, whether to get coffee before or after arriving at the office, and so on.

What we focus on in this book is not those seventy routine decisions per day, but the **Big Decisions** that affect the trajectory of your career, life, or lives of your kids. Rather than calling them "Big Decisions," I prefer to call them **Tectonic Decisions** because, like the tectonic activity of the Earth's crust, these decisions are **important, but infrequent**.

When you feel your heart racing and your palms sweating, please stop your decision-making process. This is an indication that you are approaching a Tectonic Decision.

Take a breath, review the lessons of failure contained in the following pages, and avoid the seven deadly stupidities at all costs.

Section 1: Going for the Moonshot

Genius is one percent inspiration and
99 percent perspiration.
~Thomas Edison

When we talk about a moonshot, what we really mean is not aiming high but aiming for the moon, setting objectives so high that they appear to be unattainable or, at least, unrealistic. Moonshot thinking may sound dynamic and even romantic. The problem is that emotional and impulsive thinking takes over and we buy into the "vision," whatever it may be.

Yes, some moonshots do work out, but almost all moonshots are driven by magical thinking and hoping for a perfect alignment of the stars. In reality, going for the moonshot is an extremely low-probability scenario and will likely fail.

When you examine more closely the "inventions" and "moonshots" of others, you can observe a pattern. Despite claims made by sponsors and participants, many moonshots are not moonshots at all. They are nothing more than incremental improvements on existing technologies.

Moonshots do entail risk. They are not called "freeshots." The potential financial, reputational, and other collateral damage resulting from a failed moonshot should be considered, as it could be devastating.

Most importantly, when embarking on a Tectonic Decision like a moonshot, it must be done in an environment that can not only withstand a moonshot gone wrong but also be able to fund and support the moonshot without the moonshot competing for corporate bandwidth and funding.

Chapter 1: Thomas Edison: The Light Bulb Went On

More than anything else, Thomas Edison was a good businessperson. While still in his teens, he created a mini empire selling newspapers on trains. At the age of twenty-one, he was granted his first patent for an electronic vote-counting machine to be used in counting votes in Congress. The device was a flop. The chairman of the congressional committee evaluating the new device famously said, "If there is any invention on earth that we don't want down here, that is it."

If he could only have seen 150 years into the future and been able to witness the never-ending controversy surrounding vote counting in the 2020 U.S. presidential election, but that is another story.

Edison pressed on with his side hustle of building and testing new ideas while he toiled at unexciting day jobs.

His first success was the quadraplex telegraph. It was timely, as it provided the North with a tremendous tactical advantage over the South in the Civil War. Many believe the ability of the North to quickly relay information about troop movements, weather, and other elements of battle was decisive in the outcome of the war.

Edison did not invent the telegraph. He incrementally improved a version of it that allowed multiple messages to be sent in each direction simultaneously.

After selling the quadraplex telegraph, Edison had the funds to set up shop and become a full-time inventor, which he did by creating the now-famous Thomas Edison Center at Menlo Park research laboratory in New Jersey in 1878. (Hence the Edison moniker, "The Wizard of Menlo Park.")

Until his death in 1931, Edison and his researchers were credited with more than 1,000 patents.

However, his most important invention was one that couldn't be patented: the process of modern invention itself. By applying the principles of mass production to the 19th-century model of the solitary inventor, Edison created a process in which skilled scientists, machinists, designers, and others collaborated at a single facility to research, develop, and manufacture new technologies. (Source: Thomas Edison Center at Menlo Park Museum)

Edison's factory of invention was staffed by dozens of engineers, scientists, and mathematicians. Out of this process came many of the most important inventions of modern life, including the phonograph, the electric light bulb, the kinetograph and kinetoscope (early motion picture camera and viewer), and the first alkaline battery.

But, as we further analyze Edison's production, we see that most of Edison's inventions were not wake-up-in-the-middle-of-the-night strokes of genius. He is credited for many things that involved large teams of people, and he was shrewd in gaining patents on derivatives or upgrades of existing inventions. He was also, no doubt, a genius, but also quite a businessman. After his voting machine failure, he vowed, "Anything that won't sell, I don't want to invent. Its sale is proof of utility, and utility is success."

After decades of operation, the Edison shop did produce a handful of apparent moonshots which, upon closer examination, were mostly incremental and commercial improvements to existing technologies.

Most famously, he is credited with the creation of the incandescent light bulb. The concept of incandescence means that light is created through heating an object. Think about that glowing burner on the stove; the heat is generating the light. With the light bulb, electricity runs through a filament, that wiry looking material inside the bulb, causing it to glow.

There were more than twenty other inventors who created incandescent light bulbs **before** Edison. But Edison and his army at the Menlo Park lab kept experimenting with different materials for filaments, since the burn time, or the time that light was generated, was always too short. The Edison team tested thousands of materials to **improve** on existing light-bulb technology before settling on a type of carbon that would burn for fourteen hours. Later, improvements by Edison and his team included using bamboo instead of carbon, which burned for more than a thousand hours. One of the world's most important inventions was not a moonshot after all, but rather a series of incremental improvements of an existing technology.

There is no doubt that we have a better world as a result of Edison's efforts, but should modern professionals and companies model their moonshot approaches based on the Edison system? If only they could separate themselves from the glamour and wow-factor, no contemporary technology companies would talk about moonshots and they would realize almost everything, even from the genius Thomas Edison, is an incremental improvement on something else.

Chapter 2: Google X, the Moonshot Factory

Our goal: 10x impact on the world's most intractable problems, not just 10% improvement.
~ from the Google X website

Gee, who wouldn't want to be part of that company? As we start our discussion of Google X, it seems that it has outdone Edison in the business and marketing department, announcing to the world such a lofty goal, openly disclosing the various projects underway, and speaking in cryptic language about how Google X is doing financially. The perfect illustration of the fact that going for moonshots is, well, stupid.

(Google X is not to be confused with the recent rebranding of Twitter as "X." Google X was started in 2010 and although it is now also branded as just "X," we will refer to it as "Google X" for the sake of clarity.)

I don't know about you, but if I had an idea on how to travel from New York to London in thirty minutes, I would tell nobody about it until it worked and it was ready to benefit society (and my bank account). This brings us to the motivations of Google in setting up and talking about Google X.

Astro Teller – yes, that's his real name -- is the CEO of Google X. I would label Teller as an "evangelist of failure." Teller gives TED talks and guest lectures and pontificates on radio and television about Google X and its culture, one that encourages killing projects that will not work. "We shut down more than 100 projects last year," is a typical boast from Teller.

Wow, these guys must be tough. Then again, one of the projects that was shut down was a set of contact lenses with built-in glucose monitors and another was teleportation (yeah, like on *Star Trek*). Another one was Project Loon, which used a series of high-altitude balloons to bring basic internet service to developing countries. A noble project, indeed, but there is more to a moonshot than a new technology. One of the drivers of Loon's shutdown, after eight years of trying, had nothing to do with technology and everything to do with how people live. The same illiteracy and societal barriers that stop pharmaceutical companies from airdropping life-saving medicines to developing countries plagued Loon. If the population cannot figure out how to use the medicine or follow the instructions to get on the internet, the effort is wasted.

The whole "it's okay to fail because you learn so much" mentality is bothersome to me. It is true that people who have been through failures generally have developed a better sense of whether something is going off the tracks. But creating a culture around, celebrating, and publicizing failure?

Let's go to an abstract example. In his book, *Summer of '49*, David Halberstam chronicles the 1949 New York Yankees baseball team. At that point in their history, all the Yankees did was win. In the ten seasons from 1943 to 1953, the Yankees won the World Series seven times. In the book, Halberstam gives us an inkling of what it was like to live in a winning culture, one that did not celebrate failure. He describes what happened when an outfielder dove for a ball, missed it, and returned to the dugout at the end of an inning. There were no pats on the back or chants of "nice try." Nothing was said at all. What needed to be said was already understood, *you should have caught it*.

Staying with baseball for a minute, what about Bob Gibson? Gibson pitched in the 1960s and 1970s, is a hall of famer, and considered by any baseball fan to be among best pitchers ever in baseball. In the last inning of his last game in September 1975, Gibson gave up a grand slam to Chicago Cub Pete LaCock. LaCock recalls Gibson screaming as LaCock was rounding the bases. LaCock thought Gibson was going to attack him. Some ten years later, Gibson faced LaCock in an old-timer's game. Gibson promptly drilled LaCock in the back with a fastball. Gibson shouted at LaCock, "I've been waiting years to do that."

I think if Astro Teller could interview Gibson about what he learned from his failures, Teller could wind up dismembered.

Is the team at Google X on to something or is Google X one big marketing stunt for Alphabet, the Google parent company? It looks like Google X is an attempt to divert attention from the fact that Alphabet still relies on advertising for more than 80 percent of its revenues and, despite a few decades of trying, has not been able to truly diversify its business. An unnamed executive said it well in a story on Bloomberg: "No one wants to face the reality that this is an advertising company with a bunch of hobbies."

In 2015, Ruth Porat, an accomplished financial services industry executive, joined Google as its CFO. Porat was big on accountability and divisions like Google X had to start paying for services it was getting from other Google divisions. Imagine the (fictitious) dialogue between financial disciplinarian Porat and the pony-tailed scientist Teller:

Porat: Hmm, looks like Google X lost more than $3 billion last year. Is this correct?

Teller: So what! Alphabet is awash in cash and creativity cannot be put on a timeline. Look at all the projects we killed.

Porat: I see. About that space elevator I have been reading about. When do we expect to see a financial return on it?

Teller: Financial return? Huh?

With Porat as the new fiduciary sheriff in town, it didn't take long for many Google X projects to be shut down or spun off as separate companies.

I imagine her bottom line was: If they are such good ideas, go attract your own funding for them.

One of the Google X products that did get some traction was Google Glass. Glass was the integration of a computer into eyeglasses. Why am I pointing out Glass? Because it was different than most of the other projects coming out of Google X in that Glass was not a moonshot. It was an incremental improvement on existing technologies.

Glass allowed the user to speak commands, like Siri for Apple or Alexa for Amazon, to retrieve information and display it on a head-up pair of glasses with the display appearing like those found in many automobiles. If you were watching a basketball game and wanted to know Steph Curry's three-point shooting percentage in the second half of road games, just ask and Glass would put the data in front of your eyes. I tried Glass and thought it was pretty useful. I would have liked to see it make it.

Glass was not a moonshot, but the kind of incremental innovation, not invention, that would have made Edison proud. But it was not to be. Glass was shut down after about ten years in early 2023.

Google is one of the most successful companies ever. Of the many people I know who work there, every one of them is intelligent, articulate, and interesting to be around.

We need innovation and out-of-the box thinking, but if Google can't manufacture moonshots, who can?

Chapter 3: Man In the Moonshot: Elon Musk

"When something is important enough, you do it even if the odds are not in your favor."
~ Elon Musk

Love or hate him, Elon Musk has done a lot of cool stuff. Depending on the day, he is often considered to be the richest person in the world. Early on, he merged his online payments company with another similar business and presto, PayPal was born. He was an angel investor in Tesla and went on to become its Chairman, CEO, and largest shareholder. He acquired Twitter and took it private. But most interesting to our discussion of moonshots is Space Exploration Technologies Corporation, or as it is more commonly known, SpaceX.

From the SpaceX website:

The company was founded in 2002 by Elon Musk *with the goal of reducing space transportation costs and to* colonize Mars.

I don't know about you, but this sounds like a moonshot to me. Nothing in here about incremental improvement. We're going make space travel affordable, we are going to Mars, and we will live there. Musk has been saying the same thing for more than twenty years. He has not wavered.

Since its founding, SpaceX has launched and recovered rockets big and small, has docked with the International Space Station and, in a miraculous feat of engineering, re-uses its rockets. The rockets are launched, go into orbit, complete their missions, and return to Earth to land on a platform in the middle of the ocean. We can go on about all the things that SpaceX does, but we should focus on **why** it is able to do them.

Over twenty years, billions of dollars of outside capital have been raised by the company, yet Musk still has a controlling interest. Why is this important? Unlike Alphabet, Amazon, or Microsoft, whose moonshots are under the glaring eye of its public investors, as well financial sharpshooters like Alphabet CFO Porat, SpaceX is still a private company controlled by one individual. To put it simply, at SpaceX, Musk answers to no one.

Musk had a hardcore passion to get going in the space industry and he had the money to fund it himself, which was another key distinction.

As a sidebar, I can remember George Lucas, the creator of *Star Wars*, saying he didn't want to start shooting the second set of *Star Wars* movies until he could pay for it all by himself. This would give him complete budgetary and creative freedom to pursue his moonshot without the "suits" from a studio bothering him with spreadsheets and deadlines. (This was before LucasFilms was acquired by Disney.)

Musk didn't spread his bets over dozens of potential moonshots and he was stellar at raising money at higher and higher valuations that let him retain control of the company. He handpicked a management team whose core has stayed with the company for twenty years. Contrast this to the Google X approach of preaching failure and throwing resources at hundreds of ideas.

The other primary difference in the SpaceX approach is the continued and intimate involvement of the founder and chief motivator, Musk. Sure, Musk is a brilliant promoter but once SpaceX got up and running, it dominated the launch schedule at Kennedy Space Center and garnered the lion's share of the publicity for the privatization of our space industry. The company's ongoing accomplishments serve as its marketing engine.

To think of it differently, SpaceX was set up for successful moonshots (or should they be call "MarsShots?"). Its passionate founder was heavily involved and funded much of the early and riskiest SpaceX years with his own money. Maintaining control of the company allowed Musk to set the rules. For new investors, here are the rules, take them or leave them because I have people lining up to invest.

Will SpaceX make it to Mars? I have a hard time betting against the company for the reasons stated above. Its current timeline is a Mars landing by 2029. It is interesting to note that two other new startups, Relativity Space and Impulse Space, both claim they will go to Mars in 2024. Neither has had a successful launch yet, while SpaceX has had 300 of them. Perhaps after the layoffs at Google X, its marketing people may have moved over to Relativity and Impulse.

Update

In July 2023, SpaceX raised $750 million of new capital at a valuation of $150 billion. In other words, SpaceX gave up ½ of one percent of its ownership in exchange for ¾ of a billion dollars.

In June 2024, shares of SpaceX traded privately at a valuation of $210 billion.

Chapter 4: Lonely at the Top: Lance Armstrong and Tyler Hamilton

As a teenager, Lance Armstrong was a national champion at sprint-distance triathlon and then decided to focus only on cycling. Soon thereafter, as a professional cyclist, he won the World Road Race Championship. The sky was the limit for young Armstrong.

Not long after becoming a world champion (and he was clean at this time, no performance-enhancing drugs), Armstrong received a diagnosis of testicular cancer. His medical team gave him a close to zero percent chance of living through it. But he did. And he returned to cycling.

Let's imagine that you were a world champion cyclist, defeated an impossible cancer, and then returned to competitive cycling. What would be your objective? Obviously, to win more world championships and, most of all, the biggest race, the Tour de France. In other words, a moonshot.

Armstrong is a rare example of somebody who set out on a moonshot and was justified. Think about the training and sacrifice that went into winning that first world title before his cancer.

Would he be satisfied with coming back and just being competitive, with an occasional win or third-place finish against athletes he had dominated a short time ago? No way.

Armstrong went on to win an unprecedented seven consecutive Tour de France titles.

We all know what happened that made those seven Tour de France wins possible. Armstrong was kicked out of the sport for doping and using performance-enhancing drugs. All his wins were vacated.

Was it Armstrong's greed for more wins? His fear of not winning? Perhaps he had less conscious control of his actions than he realized. (I am not an Armstrong apologist.)

Armstrong was a highly motivated individual. There are two basic types of motivation. If you are intrinsically motivated, you want to win the race because you really don't know any other way to think about it. You don't care about the medals or the prize money. If you are extrinsically motivated, you only care about the medals, prize money, and approval of others. Most of us lie somewhere in the middle. We are intrinsically motivated to succeed but won't turn down the prize money.

What happened to Armstrong?

My theory is that in his early years, he was intrinsically motivated. He wanted to be the best. He tested clean for performance-enhancing drugs and was a young man taking the sport by storm. After reaching a level of success, and the fame and fortune that went along with it, he flipped to being extrinsically motivated and did whatever he could to stay on top, including the whole doping thing.

He was still driven to win, but the prospect of not being on top and the subsequent loss of the approval of millions of fans, the cycling world and, last but not least, the sponsors, was too much.

While we hear a lot about Armstrong, professional cycling is a team sport, so Armstrong's moonshot affected many others. A cycling team consists of the team leader and the domestiques. The leader is the star of the team and the one that the domestiques support. (The word "domestique" is derived from the French word for servant.) The domestiques will form a circle around the leader to insulate him from the wind or they will chase down another team to conserve the energy of the leader.

Tyler Hamilton was one of the world's top cyclists in the 1990s and 2000s. Although Armstrong was the U.S. Postal Service team leader and Hamilton a domestique on the team, many would say that Hamilton was as good or better than

Armstrong. Hamilton was on several of the teams that drove Armstrong to all those victories in the Tour de France. Hamilton, on his own, won the 2004 Olympic gold medal.

After his Olympic win, Hamilton started failing drug tests and many of his wins were erased. Finally, in 2011, he came clean in a tell-all book titled *The Secret Race*. Hamilton admitted to doping and using banned substances throughout his career. The pressure to win was just too much for him.

Hamilton made a monumental decision to come clean. He implicated Armstrong and others with his book and pretty much brought down the cycling profession. He was a highly respected rider who had been inside the sport for a long time. He had significant credibility since he was blowing the whistle on himself as well.

What we should learn from Armstrong and Hamilton is that with any moonshot comes a great deal of risk. In the business world, it is mostly financial risk (witness the fictional conversation above between Porat and Teller of Alphabet).

In sports, and in the rest of life, the risk is different. By taking the moonshot, we are trying to distinguish ourselves or rise above the competitors. Taking shortcuts or violating real or cultural rules comes with penalties. Remember, they are not called "freeshots." Risk cannot be discounted when thinking about a moonshot.

Chapter 5: The Accidental Moonshot: Time Berners-Lee and WWW

Tim Berners-Lee is the computer scientist who invented "The World Wide Web." Yes, he literally invented it. The web is different from the Internet. Think of the Internet as a system of highways and roads that connects things together. In real life, we really don't see the Internet; it's in the background. The web is all the cool stuff we do see that is built on top of the Internet. Every website, blog, or video stream runs through the web.

Berners-Lee may have known his invention would change the world, but that is doubtful. In his autobiography, he thought the web would be a system to allow scientists to share files and use hypertext, the underlined links that we click through to see more or go to another page, to make retrieving and navigating information more efficient.

He also had a strong vision for an open web, where the free and open exchange of information would be protected and kept away from corporate or government interests that could limit the access or the information itself.

As an academic scientist, Berners-Lee wanted to improve humanity. By giving away the web, he made information-sharing easier for billions of people. A great idea, and one that was desperately needed as society was quickly moving into the information age in the 1980s.

When he made the decision to release the computer code and make the web "open source" and available to all, it rapidly grew into what we use today. Berners-Lee was first driven by the desire to improve a filing system used by fellow researchers. When he realized what www.anything.com could become, he was driven to do something to change the world. He was not driven by the desire for material personal wealth.

Imagine that?

Chapter 6: Avoiding the Stupidity of a Moonshot

Of all the things people love to talk about, moonshots are high on the list. Whether it's the bold vision to change the world by creating a new medicine or a no-carbon footprint fuel, we get romanced by the moonshot.

How many times have you been in a conversation when somebody (including yourself) can't resist mentioning the story you read about creating a settlement on one of Jupiter's moons or using sea water as jet fuel? A lot. Talking about moonshots makes us feel cutting edge and smarter than everybody else.

Don't be fooled. For every successful moonshot we hear about, there are millions that have failed and that we don't hear about. Or more precisely, how many moonshots are just enhancements to existing products or services? One of the takeaways from this chapter should be that many modest advances are slickly packaged to masquerade as moonshots.

A true and successful moonshot is tough to find these days because of the change in how information moves in our economy. More than 100 years ago, inventors were working on products to help us move information around (e.g., the telegraph), whereas today, we welcome innovations that help us filter and reduce the amount of information that we are expected to consume.

When Guglielmo Marconi was working on building the first radio in Italy, I don't think he had day-to-day updates about what was going on in Edison's lab in New Jersey. Innovators were more solitary by nature since as a species, humans were more solitary in 1900 than they are today, where everybody is connected to everything all the time. In such a connected world, it is more difficult to harness a breakaway idea into a moonshot since everybody will learn what you are doing and copy it, or worse, create a cheap knock-off that provides 80 percent of the functionality for one percent of the price.

If you or your organization has the resources to go for a moonshot, if you feel it is the right place and right time to take such a risk, and if you can withstand the fallout of a failure, then please go ahead and launch one. Most of us are not in this position. Going for a moonshot can mean financial and/or reputational ruin.

Jane: His star was rising at the company until he pushed for that proposal to build a greenhouse that would float on top of our office building.

John: What an idiot! He could have been a Vice President.

The world needs people going for moonshots. In fact, the more the better. Moonshots bring innovation and world-changing results.

Make sure you are in the right framework and position to launch a moonshot. In other words, trying for a moonshot inside of a publicly traded profit-driven enterprise is a no-win situation. You will only be known as a big spender, consumer of resources, and somebody working on a pet project of the CEO or owner.

The staff at Google X all had impeccable credentials, and that may have been the problem. If a twenty- or thirty-something Google X employee got tired of Google X failing, or when it did succeed, it didn't mean a real difference in her paycheck. What would she do? **The moonshot was interesting to her as a project, not a passion**. When it became obvious that the project was not going anywhere, then it was on to another moonshot team, or out of Google X altogether into another job at Google or at a different prestigious company.

Study after study has pointed to determination, grit, or whatever label you put on it, as the most important factor in getting a start-up, a moonshot, or similar venture to succeed, not your education, not your family's pedigree, and not how rich you are. How many of today's tech billionaire's never finished college? Most of them.

In business plans that have been presented to me that are accompanied by an ask for my investment and or involvement, I look for one thing: is there a founder that will make the necessary sacrifices to get the job done? Often, the answer is "no." But, believe me, they are all filled with wonderful-looking resumes, the names of the best schools, and the best brands in business.

With the exceptions of certain privately-owned companies like SpaceX and LucasFilms, moonshots are the province of pure venture capitalists, universities, and well-funded non-profits.

Berners-Lee worked at a non-profit organization called CERN. From the CERN website:

> CERN is a truly unique organisation. A genuine collaboration between countries, universities, and scientists, driven not by profit margins, but by a commitment to create and share knowledge.

This is a statement like those you will see at research universities and non-profits that are trying to cure cancer. While I believe most moonshots will originate in these beds of learning, make no mistake that there will be a stampede of entrepreneurs standing by to incrementally improve whatever is invented there.

Section 2: Surrendering to FOMO

FOMO. fear of missing out: fear of not being included in something (such as an interesting or enjoyable activity) that others are experiencing.
~ Merriam-Webster Dictionary

Even calloused, professional investors are susceptible to FOMO. But how can this be? If we remember the old rule of "follow the money," things will come into focus. Professional investors are charged with investing **other people's money**. These professionals have accountability not really to themselves or their dreams, but to the investors who have entrusted them with making their money grow.

Professional investors who are trying to deliver financial returns do not want to face their investors and say, "Yeah, we did miss the next big thing."

It is this dynamic that makes FOMO inevitable and almost predictably repeatable. What is even more confounding is that these investors are highly educated and sophisticated businesspeople.

The consequence is that FOMO starts small and builds to a crescendo, usually the collapse of a business and the wash-out of the investment.

It is well documented that humans are more likely to respond to fears and threats than the rewards of pleasure. Perhaps it is a primitive neurobiological reaction, but it is one that is relevant to this discussion.

Avoid situations where there is a rush to "get in" and little fear of failure. For this, you need to trigger not a reaction of exuberance, but rather that primitive reaction of fear and threat.

Think, "Why is there all this pressure to rush into this?" instead of "I better hurry to get in before I miss it," and use the fear-threat emotion to develop and refine your FOMO radar.

Chapter 7: Wonder Woman, Not: Theranos

When an uncle asked the school-aged girl what she wanted to be when she grew up, the answer from the girl was, "A billionaire." By the time the girl turned nineteen, she had dropped out of college and started her own company called Real Time Cures.

The company was built as a response to the girl's fear of needles and her desire to simplify blood testing and the all-important diagnoses that originate with testing. Real Time Cures became Theranos and Elizabeth Holmes became the world's youngest-ever, self-made billionaire.

Theranos had a young, dynamic, and photogenic founder while having the noble mission of making laboratory testing accessible and affordable for all. Holmes was an effective salesperson and prodigious fundraiser. She raised more than $900 million of venture capital for the company from a list of prominent, experienced investors. Here is some documented FOMO from *The New York Times*:

> In 2014, Dan Mosley, a lawyer and power broker among wealthy families, asked the entrepreneur Elizabeth Holmes for audited financial statements of Theranos, her blood testing start-up. Theranos never produced

any, but Mr. Mosley invested $6 million in the company anyway — and wrote Ms. Holmes a gushing thank-you email for the opportunity.

Source: "What Red Flags? Elizabeth Holmes Exposes Investors' Carelessness" by Erin Griffith, *The New York* Times, November 4, 2021

All-in, Mosely's client network of wealthy families invested almost $400 million in Theranos.

Note that these funds were "equity," not debt. Equity was not secured by buildings, land, or any other hard asset like debt. If it were debt (like a home mortgage) and the company did not make its interest payments, the issuer of the debt can seize and sell off the buildings to pay back the debt.

Equity was a bet that the value of the company would go up at some future date. The thinking was that after Theranos had proved to be successful, somebody would pay a higher price for the equity and the original investors could sell at a profit. There is a reason it is called **"venture"** capital.

In addition to the fundraising, Holmes assembled a board of directors that read like a who's who of American credibility. Board members included former Secretaries of State George Shultz and Henry Kissinger, and former Senators Bill Frist and Sam Nunn, to name a few.

Walgreens, a Fortune 100 company, rushed to make an investment and secure a deal that would put Theranos testing equipment in Walgreens stores everywhere. The Theranos relationship would help Walgreen's transform itself from being a steady, if unspectacular, drug store chain to a full-service healthcare company. With the massive foot traffic already present in its stores, Walgreens saw limitless upside in the Theranos-inside-of-Walgreens strategy.

Walgreens was suffering from a type of quick-onset FOMO. Theranos shrewdly (and appropriately) put Walgreens in the position of, "Hey, if you don't do the deal with us, we will go to CVS, Safeway, etc." This was a brilliant approach Theranos took to induce the counterparty to have a FOMO attack and sign on the dotted line.

To recap: Almost a billion dollars of equity raised, a star-studded board of directors watching over things, and one of the biggest and best-known retail footprints in healthcare signed up as an investor and key business partner.

Starting in 2015, a series of stories in *The Wall Street Journal* exposed the fact that **there was no Theranos technology** that was able to perform a staggering number of tests based on a pinprick of blood. The company was essentially a hoax.

On November 18, 2022, thirty-eight-year-old Elizabeth Holmes was convicted of four counts of criminal fraud and sentenced to more than eleven years in prison.

When it comes to an evaluation of the bad decisions around Theranos, there is much to discuss.

Let's start with the decision to invest. Many investors thoroughly research a company's industry, management team, customers, etc., but many simply follow each other into deals. It happens quickly and looks something like this:

AlphaInvestorDude: Bro, we are looking to make a big investment in this company.

RandomInvestorDude: Cool. How much of the deal can my firm get?

AlphaInvestorDude: I don't know, man. This one is really hot. I heard that MegaInvestorDude was investing as well.

RandomInvestorDude: Hey, we hooked you up last year with that company that was making a vacuum cleaner that can also be used as a blender.

AlphaInvestorDude: You're right. Me and my partners remember these things.

RandomInvestorDude: Can we get fifteen percent of the deal?

AlphaInvestorDude: Done.

RandomInvestorDude: Awesome. Oh, I hate to be a pain in the ass, but I will get questions about a few things before we can invest.

AlphaInvestorDude: Sure. Fire away.

RandomInvestorDude: What does the company do?

If we look closely at the list of Theranos investors, we can detect a pattern: Other than Tim Draper, none of the investors were traditional venture capital investors. All the others were wealthy individuals who invested through "family offices," small businesses that manage the money of wealthy families and did not have the discerning eye and structured insistence on scrutiny that venture capital has.

In other words, their investments were somewhat impulsive, like chasing after the shiniest object in the room. It should be noted that while

Draper is a hugely successful and admired venture capital investor, his firm did not invest. As a friend of the Holmes family, Draper personally invested a grand total of $1.0 million.

The most basic analysis of any investment includes a review of audited financial statements. The financial audit is performed by an outside firm and the sacred principle of objectivity is followed according to generally accepted accounting principles, or GAAP:

> The objectivity principle is the concept that the financial statements of an organization be based on solid evidence. The intent behind this principle is to keep the management team and the accounting department of an entity from producing financial statements that are slanted by their opinions and biases.

Without the audit, an investor is relying on the company's unverified representations. For example, the company may claim it sold one hundred units of its product last year. Those one hundred units may be more like fifty units sold and paid for, twenty-five units being evaluated by customers, and twenty-five more units based on a handshake the CEO made with a customer. In the opinion of management, one hundred units have been sold, but an auditor would verify the fifty sold units and that would be it.

The job of the auditor is to apply accounting standards (like defining what an actual sale is) across companies and across industries so investors and others can rely on the consistency of these definitions.

If a company does not have an audit, it is common for venture capital and other professional investors to send in a team of smart MBA types to scrub the numbers and verify management's claims (e.g., 100 units sold). In my experience, the detailed financial evaluations by professional investors are more rigorous than an audit.

In the case of Theranos, there was no audit and there was no scrubbing of the numbers by experienced financial professionals. Investors took the word of the company and Holmes about how great everything was and how incredible the future would be. You don't need this book to tell you that taking a person's word for it is a perfect recipe for a screw-up, especially one that involves large sums of money.

In fact, it was worse than not having an audit.

Here is a summary from of the testimony from the Holmes trial by Danise Yam, financial controller at Theranos:

> KPMG had decided to audit the financial information for 2009 and 2010 at the same time and produce a report covering the two years together. However, KPMG disagreed with the company about... [certain items]... The issue was never resolved, and KPMG never issued an opinion on either the 2009 or 2010 financial statements.

> Source: "Elizabeth Holmes and Her Big 4 Audit Firm Buddies at Theranos" by Francine McKenna, The Dig on Substack.com, January 6, 2022

So, it wasn't like Theranos ignored the whole audit thing. It tried to get an audit, but it could not agree with the auditors on the numbers. So, no audit.

And Walgreens still invested? FOMO.

The media also fell for the story and fell hard. One of the most respected business journalists around is Ken Auletta. He has published books on Google, Microsoft, Harvey Weinstein, Lehman Brothers, and many more. He has written dozens of articles in the *New Yorker*, *The New York Times*, and other media outlets. The thing about Auletta's writing is that people actually read his stuff and talk about it. (I have read most everything Auletta has written over the last several decades.)

Auletta did a full-length story on Holmes and Theranos in the *New Yorker*. He wrote a balanced story that extolled the virtues of Theranos – if it matured into a full-sized company – while at the same time pointing out the troubling secrecy and the lack of external industry or regulatory oversight. Upon closer examination of the story, Auletta was careful to attribute all the "change the world" statements to direct quotes from Holmes that were not supported by research. He also referenced competitors and medical experts who had expressed deep skepticism regarding the company's claims.

John Carreyrou, a reporter for *The Wall Street Journal*, read the Auletta piece on Holmes and, despite the generally positive tone of the story, sensed the hesitation of Auletta to go all-in on Theranos. Carreyrou, who was mainly working with whistleblower and a hero of the story, Tyler Shultz, went on to break the story of the Theranos fraud.

For the twenty-two-year-old Shultz in his first job, it was a huge risk. The situation was complicated by the fact that former Secretary of State George Shultz, and Tyler's grandfather, sat on the Theranos board. Tyler provided information to Carreyou about the "open secret" inside the company that nothing really worked. When Tyler was exposed as a source for Carreyrou, he felt the full force of Holmes and her army of lawyers and nearly exhausted his family's resources to fund his own defense.

Yet, he did not waiver and, in large part, is responsible for potentially saving countless lives that could have been affected by flawed Theranos testing.

> "John Carreyrou did a brilliant job of exposing Elizabeth Holmes — I did not," Auletta reflected. "So, when I look back on that, yeah, I did a profile of her, but I did not produce the goods that he did."

> Source: "Ken Auletta: Eilzabeth Holmes 'Gave Me Gobbledygook" by Dylan Croll, Yahoo!Finance, October 20, 2022

Writers across the business and social world fawned over the young entrepreneur. *Fortune* Magazine, *Time, Inc.*, and all the rest of them believed Holmes at her word.

Once Carreyrou broke the story, the media praise shifted from Holmes to Carreyrou and Shultz. From John Naughton in *The Guardian*:

Eventually, Theranos came to be valued at $10bn, which gave Holmes a net worth of several billion and made her the youngest self-made female billionaire in history. It also made her perfect glossy magazine-cover material: just think – a glamorous, single, smart young woman set on changing the world using digital technology.

There was, however, one fly in the lip gloss – a grizzled *Wall Street Journal* investigative reporter, name of John Carreyrou. Alerted by a whistleblower, he started digging and discovered that the Theranos pitch was baloney. The vaunted kit either didn't work or produced wacky results. It had never undergone any independent, peer-reviewed testing. Some of the demonstrations were faked by having the blood samples covertly tested on conventional machines.

Source: "How Theranos Used the Media to Create the Emperor's New Start-Up" by John Naughton, *The Guardian, June 3, 2018*

This goes back to the question of a biased media (more on this in Section 5: Trusting the Media). Objectivity and balance do not get page views. As described by Naughton above, the Holmes story was a great story. Why screw it up with messy details like checking to see if the product actually worked?

Jean-Louis Gassée, former senior executive at Apple, did just that. (Source: "Theranos Trouble: A First Person Account" by Jean-Louis Gassée, Monday Note on Medium, October 18, 2015)

He had his blood tested at a Stanford University lab then walked down the street to Walgreens and had the Theranos tests done. By now, you can guess the outcome: Two rounds of tests from the Stanford lab (after all, the guy had degrees in math and physics) and two rounds of results from Theranos that were not close to the values from Stanford. As he said, "Which should I believe?" Gassée, like most of us, would say that the Stanford results were based on billions of samples running through a lab process that has been around for dozens of years is the choice over a startup that uses a black box to spit out results.

Gassée was no genius. Well, in fact he was, but he was not a medical expert or a journalist. He was somebody who stayed with his rigorous decision-making process and did not buy into the hype.

We could say that Gassée has excellent FOMO radar.

Chapter 8: Venture Bros Gone Wild: Webvan

Before DoorDash, GrubHub, and Instacart, there was Webvan. Webvan was a grocery delivery business, but not from your local stores. It was founded in 1996 by Louis Borders, who also founded Borders Books, a successful business in the pre-Amazon era.

Webvan contracted for more than $1 billion with Bechtel, one of the largest engineering companies in the world, to build automated Webvan warehouses in cities across the U.S. to store all those steaks, apples, and milk before orders were placed and deliveries made.

The warehouses used state-of-the-art technology to manage inventory and load delivery trucks. Webvan's promise was there was no need to deal with the hassle of the grocery store when you can place your order and get it all within thirty minutes.

Webvan secured almost $400 million of funding from a list of initial investors that read like a big money all-star team:

- Sequoia Capital
- Goldman Sachs
- Softbank Capital
- Benchmark Capital

On top of that, Webvan poached George Shaheen from his perch, literally on top of the business world, as the head of Andersen Consulting, now known as Accenture, to be its CEO.

A few short years later in 1999, Webvan went public, raising an additional $375 million. At the point of going public, Webvan had a few hundred thousand dollars in sales and tens of millions in annual losses. The valuation of the company at the end of its first day of trading was $8 billion.

With almost $800 million in capital raised, a monster IPO valuation, and one of the world's most respected business leaders as CEO, what could go wrong? After less than two years of operations, Webvan filed for bankruptcy in 2001.

The idea for Webvan was a good one. This was proven fifteen years later by the success of the "Delivery 2.0" companies, DoorDash, GrubHub, Instacart, and others, with the premise being that consumers would trade a little extra money for the cost of the delivery service for the time it saved them by avoiding the grocery store.

The execution was also good at Webvan. The warehouses and trucks did, in fact, deliver on the Webvan business proposition of delivery within thirty minutes.

So, what went wrong?

As the saying goes, "Follow the money." The money in this case originated from venture capital investors.

Venture capital is a type of private equity financing that is provided to early stage, high-potential, growth companies in exchange for an ownership stake in the company. Venture capital funds invest money in these companies in exchange for a percentage of the ownership and they generally have a hands-on approach to helping their companies grow and succeed. The goal of venture capital is to invest in companies with a potential for high returns and to help those companies grow so they can eventually go public or be acquired. This is a high-risk, high-reward type of investment.

Venture investing is not for the faint of heart. Harvard Business School professor Shikhar Ghosh estimates that 75 percent of venture-backed companies fail. Other conversations I have had with venture capitalists over the years go something like this:

If we make twenty investments out of a $500 million fund, we expect to have fourteen or fifteen failures that result in the complete loss of these investments, two or three that return the original investment, and one or two that make so much money that they pay back ALL the money invested by the fund, plus a healthy return. (These portfolio success ratios are similar to what I have heard from movie studios: one big hit covers all the failures.)

The upshot? Long odds and huge paybacks for the winners.

Webvan had some of the key characteristics of a successful venture investment:

- A proven founder. Borders previously built the second-largest bookseller in the world.
- A large market. Food. What more needs to be said? Is there a bigger market anywhere?
- Technology edge. Everything was automated and way more efficient than the existing grocery business.
- First mover. At the time, venture investing that involved the internet was a land grab. Get there first, like Amazon or eBay, and you can own the market.

Webvan started in the San Francisco Bay Area and was targeted at households that had disposable income but were pressed for time.

Kevin LaBuz summarizes the strategy:

The Webvan Group planned to begin by offering groceries that people shop for frequently to build critical mass, order frequency, and economies of scale. With an established customer base, it then planned to leverage its distribution system to expand to other categories, adding items such as consumer electronics and books whose profit margins were considerably greater than for groceries but were ordered less frequently. That is, they planned to attract an audience first and then "monetise those eyeballs" to bring in additional revenue and do this on a global scale.

Source: "#129 – Back to the Future – Webvan" by Kevin LaBuz, Substack, June 26, 2022

Around the time of the Webvan launch, my family relocated to the Bay Area and became Webvan customers. One night, as I was finishing a Webvan order on the computer for the week's supply of peanut butter, bread, and chicken, I was called away for a phone call. Upon my return twenty minutes later, I noticed my enterprising four-year-old son sitting at the computer. Once he saw me, he jumped and took off.

As I re-engaged with my mundane grocery order, I noticed my shopping cart now had more than $4,000 worth of items in it. As I went through the details of the cart, I observed that my son had added a few televisions, various sound system components, remote-controlled racing cars, and several other high-ticket items which, for Webvan, were items that made ten times more profit margin than groceries. So, I was being monetized by Webvan, according to its plan, but not according to my budget.

Webvan's pricing was competitive with grocery stores, and that may have been the problem. With its ever-expanding array of warehouses being built at $30 to $40 million a pop, Webvan was creating a massive fixed-cost infrastructure, which is no problem if you have the profit margins and the volumes. Grocery stores have average profit margins of one to three percent. By comparison, software and technology companies (which Webvan thought it was) have margins of more than 25 percent. As a result of its fixed costs and pricing its products to be competitive, Webvan faced the desperate task of building volumes fast enough to avoid running out of cash.

Imagine the dialogue:

Bossman: Wow, our busiest month ever. How much did we sell last month?

CubicleGuy: $15,000.

Bossman: Great news. Seems like our location will be the top profit center at Webvan this month. Right?

CubicleGuy: Well, the cost of the groceries was $14,775, so we made $225 of operating profit selling groceries.

Bossman: Oh. That's still good, isn't it?

CubicleGuy: The cost of the warehouse building and parking lot was $5,000 and the interest costs on the loans for all the conveyor belts and packing machines was $10,000. Oh, and the cost of the truck fleet was another $5,000.

Bossman: So, what are you saying?

CubicleGuy: We lost almost $20,000 last month and we had record volumes.

Bossman: Hmmm. What do you think the best font is for a resumé?

Webvan rushed into new geographic markets before it had fully proven and tested its business model in its initial market.

According to consulting firm Gartner Group:

A proof of concept is a demonstration of a product, service or solution in a sales context. A proof of concept should demonstrate that the product or concept will fulfill customer requirements while also providing a compelling business case for adoption.

For an experienced team, demonstrating proof of concept for Webvan would not have been all that hard with a couple of good diagrams showing how supplies would be purchased, how the warehouse would store items, and how deliveries would be loaded and sent to customers.

The random element in all of this was the Internet. At the time, the Internet was a new and vast frontier. It was going to change everything, everywhere, overnight. (The Internet did change everything, everywhere. But it did not happen overnight.) With a huge market, Internet technology, and a solid proof of concept – I'm ready to invest.

In the eyes of venture investors, the magnitude of change that the Internet could catalyze was staggering. There was constant talk of "disintermediation" or cutting out the middleman from all things from buying houses, placing stock trades, and feeding your pets. Slowly, but surely, venture investors, who earn their money for deliberate, calculated decision-making, were allowing their impulses to dictate decisions. Call it Internet-driven FOMO.

After proof of concept, a nascent company must decide between GBF or MVP. GBF is the acronym for Get Big Fast and MVP stands for Minimum Viable Product. With the rush to leverage its first-mover advantage and encouragement from deep-pocketed investors, Webvan went the GBF route.

> Bossman: Let's map out the strategy for entering ten more markets in the next six months.

> CubicleGuy: But we aren't fully launched yet in our first market, and this is a market where we all live.

> Bossman: Let me explain something to you, son. With the Internet, we need to move at lightning speed. If we are not fast, there are going to be many others that want to spend a billion dollars on warehouses and trucks and get there before us.

CubicleGuy: I thought the Internet was going to make brick-and-mortar business models obsolete.

Bossman: Yes, but we will have such a first-mover advantage, nobody will even try to compete with us since we will own the market.

CubicleGuy: Are we sure that the local grocery stores are not going to compete with us and start deliveries on their own?

Bossman: Won't matter. We will have miles of conveyor belts, automated systems, fleets of trucks, and our unique-looking bins. Let's get big fast and everything else will work out.

Had the company gone for an MVP, the story may have turned out differently. According to Gartner Group:

> A minimum viable product (MVP) is the release of a new product (or a major new feature) that is used to validate customer needs and demands prior to developing a more fully featured product. To reduce development time and effort, an MVP includes only the minimum capabilities required to be a viable customer solution.

If Webvan had taken the MVP route, it may have looked at a short list of products that included household staples like milk, butter, and cooking supplies, rather than include tricky items like fruits and vegetables that consumers prefer to see and touch before purchase. It may have looked at one neighborhood in the Bay Area and had one or two trucks and a warehouse that was not fully automated with five miles of conveyor belts as its Oakland warehouse had. Perhaps add a senior manager who had retail grocery experience. (None of the senior team at Webvan had grocery experience.)

First mover advantage (its own specialized type of FOMO), Get Big Fast, and the promise of new Internet technologies ruled the day and pushed the company forward using a flawed strategy for its expansion.

Michael Moritz of Sequoia Capital is one of the most successful investors of the last fifty years. His investments have included Google, Yahoo!, and PayPal, to name a few. Sequoia invested in Webvan, and Moritz was on the board.

According to Moritz on SubStack:

Webvan committed the cardinal sin of retail, which is to expand into a new territory -- before we had demonstrated success in the first market. In fact, we were busy demonstrating failure in the Bay Area market while we expanded into other regions.

Source: "#129 – Back to the Future – Webvan" by Kevin LaBuz, Substack, June 26, 2022

To be more scientific in the Webvan autopsy, we should note that the company's cost structure prevented it from making money unless it had enormous volumes. How did the company try to attract those volumes? It expanded, but it did not work out like you might think.

According to Statista, when Webvan launched, the San Francisco Bay Area had the highest per capita income in the U.S. at $72,000. What a great market! – filled with busy people with lots of disposable income.

The Bay Area would have been a good starting point if the product's geographic market had been confined to just that area. Many of the assumptions about how much and how often people would use the service were based on the Bay Area starting point.

Bossman: Looks like we are selling an average of $200 per order so far in the Bay Area market.

CubicleGuy: Yes.

Bossman: Based on this, we should project $250 per order in our next market (Charlotte, NC), since our warehouses will be running better, and we will have the kinks worked out of the system.

CubicleGuy: My mom lives in Charlotte and an extravagant spend for her is bowling night. I think she drives twenty minutes to get gas that is fifteen cents a gallon cheaper than near her house.

Bossman: Details, details. She'll be more than happy to pay a few extra dollars for the convenience we offer.

As it turns out, CubicleGuy was right again. The problem was that Charlotte, NC, was the city with the tenth highest income per capita in the U.S. at $39,000, compared with $72,000 for San Francisco. And it was all downhill from there as you moved through the rest of the country, with busy people without much disposable income when compared to the initial market.

Since its investors were convinced that Webvan was going to be **that** investment that could pay back the entire fund plus a profit, Webvan's rapid expansion was fueled by more dollars from its investors who thought, hey, let's double down on a winner.

As Webvan tried to morph from a niche service offered in the most affluent market in the U.S. to a mass market that did not have the socio-demographic profile of the Bay Area, it hit the wall. As the uptake in new markets never really materialized, investors changed their minds. After just nineteen months of operations, they did not want to throw good money after bad and stopped funding the business.

Investor indifference, a terrible way for a company to die.

Afterword

The Webvan.com domain was purchased by Amazon in 2009. Amazon hired four senior executives from Webvan as it subsequently built its AmazonFresh grocery business. In 2013, Amazon acquired Kiva Systems, the robotics company that was built to automate the Webvan warehouses. AmazonFresh spent five years only operating in the Seattle market before expanding to Los Angeles. After patiently proving out the AmazonFresh business model and becoming an expert in the food business (and not succumbing to FOMO), Amazon went all-in and acquired Whole Foods for $13.7 billion in 2017.

Chapter 9: Pied Piper of Crypto: Sam Bankman-Fried

Alameda Research was a crypto trading operation. It`risked money on sophisticated crypto trades. It was Alameda's inability to realize that its business and trading model was flawed that led to the multi-billion-dollar collapse of crytpo exchange FTX and the arrest of its 30-year-old founder, Sam Bankman-Fried or as he is known, SBF.

Alameda played a high-stakes game. For example, rather than using a traditional investing style where Alameda would buy Bitcoin at a low price and then sell it at a higher price, Alameda specialized in arbitrage.

In an arbitrage trade, the trader takes advantage of small price differences in an asset like Bitcoin. These price differences might be Bitcoin trading at $20,000 on an exchange in Asia when compared with $20,100 on an exchange in Europe. Buy Bitcoin in Asia and immediately sell it in Europe to lock in a profit. To make that $100, $20,000 had to be put at risk for seconds or minutes.

Arbitrage is more fruitful when dealing with less-popular assets as the markets for these are generally less efficient, meaning price differences can exist between crypto exchanges, if only briefly. Think about it as if you have the only lemon tree on the block and want to charge $2 per lemon. People can pay you the $2 or walk a mile to the next lemon tree and pay $1, or they just don't know what pricing is outside of your offer of $2 per lemon. Alameda used powerful computers to search for, find, and buy those other lemons for $1 and sell them at $2.

Arbitrage traders take advantage of these small price inefficiencies, which may last only seconds, to make big bets and lock in a profit. So, if Alameda had such a good thing going, why did its founders start FTX??

FTX did what was – yawn -- pretty close to what goes on in the world of stocks, bonds, and retirement accounts at places like Merrill Lynch, TD Ameritrade, and Charles Schwab. Not all that exciting, but these institutions act as fiduciaries for its customers' funds, meaning that they are **trusted** with the safekeeping of customers' funds.

Based on my own experience in crypto arbitrage, I have a theory about how the market moved around on Alameda, creating the problems that ultimately led to the bankruptcy of FTX.

As discussed above, arbitrage trading is based on market inefficiencies and the ability to capture a profit quickly. When Alameda was formed in 2017, crypto was not quite as "mainstream" as it is today. Young and "brilliant" MIT graduate SBF was not in the business news every week and crypto Super Bowl ads did not show up until a few years later. Think about our lemon example above: in the early days of the Alameda arbitrage operation, buyers and sellers did not have "perfect" information. There were information gaps that could be exploited.

From the time Alameda originated, the crypto market started rapidly gaining participants while trading volumes were exploding. Total crypto transactions went from about $34 billion per month in December 2018 to more than $2.2 trillion per month in May 2021, an increase of 65 times.

From the tops of mountains, we could hear the cries of FOMO, FOMO, FOMO.

From our basic training in economics, if a market has more participants and there is more knowledge about that market, the market will become more efficient, which means that buyers and sellers can more easily establish a clearing price where the bid (what the buyer is willing to pay) is close to the ask (what the seller is willing to take). If there were suddenly hundreds of people buying and selling your lemons and the lemons from a mile away, the $2 price and the $1 price would likely converge to around $1.50.

This is what I think happened at Alameda: As trading volumes and the number of market participants surged, the small price spreads that previously worked for Alameda slowly evaporated. In this theory, the basis for the Alameda business model changed and the adjustment was not to move on but rather to increase the size of the trades and funding them by creating a new pocket of money (FTX). Although it needed much more capital, Alameda continued make a profit on the smaller and smaller price gaps. Remember the Bitcoin example above? Well, now Alameda was only making $50 by risking $20,000, so to make that same $100, it needed to risk $40,000 (two times the $20,000).

> TraderBro1: Dude, we are killing it buying Bitcoin in Asia and selling in Europe.
>
> TraderBro2: Yeah, these new computers let us get this done before the price differences evaporate.
>
> TraderBro1: Tell me about it. Last year, the price gaps were measured in minutes. Now, with all the newbies trading like crazy, the price gaps between exchanges are only for a few seconds.
>
> TraderBro2: And the price gaps are getting smaller each day.

TraderBro1: With the price gaps so small and the trading windows so tight, we need like 10x more capital to buy and sell more crypto just to make the same profit we did last year.

TraderBro2: Man, margins have gone done the drain.

TraderBro1: Where can we get access to a big pool of capital?

FTX was most likely born to provide capital to shore up Alameda. So, rather than change the business model at Alameda, management simply threw more money at a trading operation that was based on a market theory that was quickly heading into obsolescence. Crypto arbitrage just did not work anymore, but SBF -- as the anointed young genius of crypto -- could still raise FOMO-driven money.

Once Alameda drained the FTX piggy bank -- trading more capital in a market with dwindling arbitrage margins -- FTX was unable to meet its own customers' demands for withdrawals and almost overnight, FTX was in bankruptcy.

But wait, there's more! Bankruptcy is a process to essentially sell off a company's assets (buildings, cars, stock holdings, etc.) to pay off the company's liabilities (think "paying off the mortgage"). Once in bankruptcy, a new management team is appointed to sell off assets and pay off liabilities and return customers' funds in an orderly manner.

The problem with FTX was the internal record keeping was so poor or non-existent that the new managers could not even figure out what assets and liabilities FTX even had.

Imagine the scenario when the new managers took over:

> Bossman: Okay, guys, let's first determine how much cash we have so we can start returning funds to customers.

> CubicleGuy: Um, there is no central tracking of cash.

> Bossman: No problem. Just add up what's in all the company's bank accounts.

> CubicleGuy: Um, there is no list of bank accounts.

I think you get the picture. An entire professional bankruptcy management team spent months just trying to determine how much cash FTX had – and this was a multi-billion-dollar organization.

Were there plenty of red flags that FTX was headed for trouble? Certainly. But what the media focused on was its boy-wonder founder and the great things he was doing in charitable circles, with his illicit gains, as well as his scooping up of other companies in his industry. Everybody was too busy anointing SBF as the Warren Buffett of crypto without looking under the covers. The media appealed to our impulses and emotions, which by now, you know is bad news for decision-making and an accelerant to the FOMO fire.

Chapter 10: Avoiding the Stupidity of FOMO

Fear of Missing Out is to blame for many failures, including Theranos and FTX. The lesson here is not that either company was a fraud, but rather why so many otherwise smart, certifiably accomplished, and wealthy people fell for it.

FOMO creates big-time decision-making problems. Do you want to be the one who passed up investing $100 in the next Google or Facebook? Of course not, especially when that $100 could turn into $1 million in a few years. When you feel the peer or other pressure to "get on the bandwagon," be like Apple scientist Gassée. Develop FOMO radar. Look for FOMO, sense it, and know it is happening. Then, as fast as you can, run the other way.

If you are building a new product or service, slow down, consolidate your gains, and make sure your foundation is rock solid. If you are rushing to beat a competitor to market, remember there will be more competitors coming soon, and you may have already lost the race. Pivot to a direction where there is more space to freely roam or align with an organization that has resources you don't have so you can stick it out and not be looking over your shoulder every day.

Stay away from the impulsive behavior of Webvan's investors. Initially, the Webvan investors were thoughtful and rigorous in their thinking about bringing a potentially revolutionary service to market. They shifted to impulsive, and almost panic-like thinking as they poured money into a failing business. This is classic FOMO-driven behavior.

I'm sure you have heard this before: If it's too good to be true, it's not. Collectively, billions of dollars were lost because of new and fantastic promises made by SBF in a nascent industry where there were few rules and minimal oversight. Nobody paid attention to understanding that FTX was intimately linked to Alameda. It took a day or two for the new bankruptcy management team to describe FTX as an entity that shuffled assets from fiduciary accounts at FTX over to the Alameda trading operation.

This is a type of FOMO I call the "Pied-Piper Effect." SBF and Holmes were young, smart, and persuasive. They both claimed to be breaking new ground and changing the world.

These should be the first triggers of your FOMO radar. "We are doing something that has never been done before!" Zig when others zag. When others are emphatic and so sure of themselves, this should be a trigger to pop up the FOMO radar. Once activated, your radar should transform your attitude from exuberance to skepticism.

In the aftermath of the FTX debacle, it came to light that none other than musical artist Taylor Swift turned down a $100 million promotional deal from FTX. She and her team asked a few diligence questions about the nature of crypto and of FTX's treatment of securities laws. She passed on the deal. She did not surrender to FOMO and follow the Pied Piper but went against the grain and asked a few of the right questions.

Taylor Swift is a mega rockstar and global phenomenon like few others. But to me, she is an example of somebody with excellent FOMO radar.

Section 3: Relying On Family and Friends

Don't rely on people.
~ Joel Osteen

Advice from family and friends often puts us in an awkward position. Think of it like a logic equation:

- If you follow the advice and things work out, it's a good outcome.
- If you follow the advice and things don't work out, it's a bad outcome.
- If you don't follow the advice, someone will be upset with you and that is also a bad outcome.

While it certainly matters which family member or which friend provides the advice, only one of the outcomes works out in a positive manner. Nevertheless, most of us are dealing with the "advice" problem on a regular basis, especially if you are a young person who wants to go to college.

A generation ago, it was easy for a family or friend to help a young person get into a college or get that first job. A couple of phone calls, reminders of favors to be traded, and Uncle Pete took care of it. Those days are long gone. There is now global competition for every admissions slot at every good college and for any decent entry-level job.

The proliferation of the information economy has made Uncle Pete all but obsolete. How many times have you heard that if you apply to Uncle Pete's alma mater, that his recommendation letter will be the "tiebreaker" should you be equivalent to other qualified candidates? Don't buy this.

Admissions and hiring committees are under intense scrutiny because of the free flow of information that did not exist back in the day of paper applications and in-person interviews. Resumes, background checks, scrapes of social media sites, etc., are all a few clicks on the computer that all but make Uncle Pete's endorsement meaningless.

Further, most advice from family and friends is unresearched and biased. *I went to that college and things were great.*

Where is the analysis of majors, graduation rates, alumni success, etc.? Usually, there is none of it. So, it's just an older, and therefore presumed wiser, family member or friend not giving thoughtful, up-to-date, and researched advice, but rather providing an opinion. Not a good basis for a Tectonic Decision.

Chapter 11: Going to College: Tiger Mom vs Rational Mom

How do people make the decision on whether to go to college and, if so, what college to select? As we shape our thinking to avoid a bad decision and a stupidity trap, let's build a fact base from the National Center for Education Statistics.

In the U.S., approximately 3.6 million students graduate from high school each year. Of those graduates, about 40 percent go on to four-year colleges or universities and approximately 20 percent attend two-year colleges, but that decision is far less costly and disruptive. (We are excluding two-year degree seekers from this analysis.)

With a pool of 3.6 million graduates and a 40 percent application rate to four-year colleges, that leaves us with about 1.4 million students applying to college each year. Colleges received about 12 million applications in 2021 for an average of 8.6 applications per student, up from 6.7 applications per student in 2014.

Now that we are talking about the select pool of students applying to four-year colleges (8.6 of them each, mind you), here is a statistic from AdmissionsOnly.com that will surprise you:

More than 30 percent of enrollees at four-year colleges do not make it to the second semester.

That's almost one out of every three go home for winter break during freshman year and do not return. Certainly, there are many good reasons for such a failure rate, e.g., family circumstances, illness, etc. But one out of three?

And how about this? More than 50 percent of college freshmen do not get through the initial or "weed-out" classes in their initial fields of study. That's a lot of people switching majors.

What this tells us is there are large groups of students and families that had a seriously deficient decision-making process for a decision that would likely determine the trajectory of a person's entire life, a Tectonic Decision, if there ever was one.

A generation ago, if a student had one or two Advanced Placement (AP) exams under her belt, she was considered extraordinary. At a typical "most selective" college today, the average student granted admission has ten or more AP exams completed. Ten AP exams is the equivalent of ten college courses, or a full year of study. Top students are entering college with sophomore or higher standing and finishing in two to three years.

Even with all those honors high school classes, extracurricular activities, AP tests, back-breaking college essays, recommendations, and advice from family and friends, the failure rate was high because the input factors into the decision were wrong.

How do we get to such a place?

> TigerMom: Well, now that you have finished your sophomore year of high school, it's time to start visiting colleges.

> JuniorGirl: I can't wait. Did you see the pictures in the brochure for Uptown College? The campus looks awesome.

> TigerMom: Okay. We are going to visit ten colleges over three weeks this summer. I want you to be able to make a good choice when the time comes.

So, what is going on here? JuniorGirl has not yet applied to any colleges, does not have a clue as to whether she will be admitted, but TigerMom is lining up the visits. Is it some kind of psychological torture for JuniorGirl?

You better get into one of these places, whether you like it or not.

In this scenario, the college visits happen, notes are taken, and carefully orchestrated onsite "research" is completed at each college during the twelve to twenty-four hours the student is in the vicinity of the campus.

TigerMom: So, what did you think of Uptown?

JuniorGirl: It was awesome!

TigerMom: What did you like most?

JuniorGirl: The buildings had great air conditioning. It will be really easy to study when it's hot.

TigerMom: I know! It will be so much nicer than when I went there. What else?

JuniorGirl: The tour guide was so knowledgeable about the school, and she was only a sophomore. The picnic and ice cream we had in the quad were beautiful. It was so nice out.

TigerMom: And how about that brand new athletic center with all those treadmills and Pelotons?

JuniorGirl: I know! We were only on campus for three hours. We didn't sit in on any classes, didn't talk to freshmen who would be in my major, didn't spend any time with a student advisor talking about the required core classes for all students, and didn't look at the classes required to graduate in my major, but I just know Uptown is the place for me.

I can go on, but the college-visit process introduces a staggering amount of bias into the college-decision process. So much so, that there is a better scenario:

RationalMom: Well, JuniorGirl, I see you are delivering some good grades. Keep it up and you will have many choices for where to go to college.

JuniorGirl: Cool! Can we do some college visits this summer?

RationalMom: Why would we do that? How about you concentrate on keeping up the grades and submitting strong applications? You will be notified of where you are admitted in January of senior year and have until May to make a selection, which leaves us five months to make visits.

JuniorGirl: So, do the research to figure out which schools offer courses of study that fit my academic interests? And which will give me the best shot at a job or graduate school?

RationalMom: That's right, then you send in applications.

JuniorGirl: Okay. So, I get into some colleges, go visit, and then see which one is best for me. Doing it this way, I will already be admitted to any of the schools we visit, so I know the academics will provide me with the best educational value. If there is a decent pizza place on campus, that's a bonus.

RationalMom: Exactly. Say we visit five colleges right now. If we drive and stay in basic hotels, we will spend several thousand dollars. The average college application fee was less than $50 last year. How about you research a wider variety of colleges and apply to a few more? Seems like a logical investment trade-off: spend an extra few hundred dollars to apply to more schools and increase the chances of landing some place that will work for you, compared with spending thousands hopscotching through a bunch of short visits to schools that may all reject you.

The question is: why does the approach taken by RationalMom seem like such an outlier? Two words: Rick Singer.

Buying Happiness: Rick Singer

Singer was part of the ever-growing, bias-creating, and decision-distorting college-counselor industry. With legitimate college counselors, you pay a fee for the hands-on assistance of the counselor to help your child put his best foot forward on college applications, a legitimate service for the one percent who can afford it.

Singer took it one giant step farther. He brokered admissions deals between desperate parents and coaches and administrators at colleges. Example:

> *Singer makes a deal with the soccer coach at a college for the coach to tag an applicant as "high value" or "must have" for the soccer team. If the student gains admission, Singer obtains a "fee" or "donation" from the parent, pays off the coach, and keeps a cut for himself.*

TigerMom: Let's take pictures of you kicking the soccer ball around in the yard.

JuniorGirl: Really? I hate sports, sweat, and all that stuff. That's for my brother, Mom, not me. I read books and volunteer at the homeless shelter.

TigerMom: Oh, I know, but how about a few pictures? And put on your brother's high-school soccer team jersey.

JuniorGirl: Fine. But this is weird, Mom.

Many times, unbeknownst to JuniorGirl, TigerMom would send the pictures to Singer along with a substantial cash payment. JuniorGirl would get an admissions-committee endorsement from the soccer coach and get into the school.

I know this sounds crazy, but this really happened many times over at well-known schools around the country. I had a friend with high school and college-age children at the time. He lived in a wealthy neighborhood on the West Coast, a prime target market for Singer. He said to me, "Everybody around here is nervous as hell about the Singer thing and hoping the FBI doesn't show up at their front door."

The Singer Scandal ruined many lives. Some say the parents, all whom were one-percenters, deserved the fines and prison time, but what about the students? Most of them had no idea that any of this was happening. How about the cases of students who were college juniors or seniors when it came to light that their admissions were tainted?

This goes well beyond getting advice from family and friends. It is, in a word, criminal. Parents Gone Wild might be a funny title for all this if it weren't so sad. Is a child's college process really a steppingstone for parents to improve their own social status and brag about how their child was admitted to, or more likely, visited a top school?

Uptown College vs State U.

There are other reasons the prevailing approach is problematic. Many parents believe if their child gets into a good school, the child's life is set. So, there is a feverish determination to "help" the child to get in, as in the Rick Singer example above.

Despite all the parental helicoptering, private tutors, and college coaches, average standardized test scores for the ACT and SAT have barely budged over the last several decades.

Imagine the chatter at the local grocery store:

TigerMom: I'm so relieved JuniorGirl got into Uptown College as an English major. Uptown is one of the most prestigious liberal arts schools in the country. I feel a giant weight lifted from my shoulders.

RationalMom: Really? I thought JuniorGirl was the one applying.

TigerMom: Well, you know how it is. I had to pretty much write all her essays and do half the application for her. She is just so busy with the baking club and that independent research project she is doing on the history of the Wheel of Fortune television show.

RationalMom: Oh. Why is she doing that stuff?

TigerMom: These are the things that got her in. Now that she's in, her life is set!

Since there is so much focus on "getting in," many miss the forest for the trees.

Let's ask the following question:

Which is more valuable to the student and her career after college: A liberal arts degree from a highly selective school, of which there are about two dozen in the U.S., or a STEM degree, in Science, Technology, Engineering, or Math, from the state university?

Here are a couple of stats from a survey performed by Unbound, an educational consulting firm. ("Yes" answers are the percentages.)

Are you satisfied with your current salary?
Liberal Arts 54%   STEM 77%

Did your degree prepare you for your job?
Liberal Arts 59%.   STEM 82%

There are more data out there describing the chasm between technical and non-technical majors and make no mistake, the world does need non-technical majors graduating into the work force. But as society has become dependent on the Internet and the free flow of information, technical majors are getting the jobs that pay more and offer higher job satisfaction. Revenge of the nerds.

What does this mean for the TigerMom exhorting and cajoling her child to get into a "top school?" The numbers say there is a strong probability of disappointment. A liberal arts degree from a highly selective school is theoretically better than one from a less selective school, but what is going on out there is the software engineer from Anywhere U. is happier and making more money than the humanities major from Harvard.

Look around your own circle of family and friends and do an honest evaluation. This is not a hard and fast rule but an emerging trend that is taking hold, and one that should be factored into the college-decision process.

Should the admissions process be harder than the coursework?

I have a friend who is an admissions officer at a most selective college. (Full Disclosure: None of my children applied there.) As my oldest hit eleventh grade, I asked my friend for general advice about the college application process.

Her response was amazing in its simplicity:

- Don't overdue the essay. We have seen every essay that any student could ever write. With rare exceptions, it will be hard to distinguish yourself as an applicant based on the essay.

- Take some college courses instead of AP classes. Completing real college classes while in high school will give the admissions committee confidence that the student can handle college-level work, regardless of what his inflated high school GPA says or how you can overstudy or be over-tutored to pass an AP exam.

Rather than vigorously dispensing her advice, TigerMom should consider this approach since there are so many negative side effects to the TigerMom-driven college application process.

According to an interview with Yale English professor William Deresiewicz on Goop:

> The problem is that the admissions system itself has gotten so confusing and extreme that in the course of giving your kid a better chance to get into an elite college, it's all probably also making them miserable, anxious, and stressed. The pressure robs them of much of what is fun and joyful about being a kid and a teenager, and also a lot of what's necessary psychologically and socially for them to develop into happy, healthy adults. They are missing out on what is ultimately going to be good not only for them but also for the people around them over the course of their lives.

Further supporting the Deresiewicz point of view is Madeline Levine, a Ph.D. clinical psychologist.

The title of her book says it all:

The Price of Privilege: How Parental Pressure and Material Advantage Are Creating a

Generation of Disconnected and Unhappy Kids

In her book, Levine details the unhealthy and nearly toxic relationship many upper-middle class parents have with their children. TigerMom can sum this up for us:

> TigerMom: We want you to be happy, as long as you get the highest grades in all of the top classes.
>
> JuniorGirl: Oh, but I want to be in the school play and that means I can't take that honors science class.
>
> TigerMom: Life is all about choices and if you want to make that choice today, you should think about what that means for your future.

In her insightful post Nicole LaPorte explains how the college admission process has changed over the last decade to be more democratic and "fair" to more applications.

This has created a dilemma now facing upper-middle class families (like TigerMom's) that are used to getting their way:

> To try to fit themselves into this new world order, affluent families are rethinking their

admissions strategies. Gone are the letters of recommendation from a family-friend-slash-CEO or celebrity. As another Los Angeles parent told me, "A letter from a fancy person is not going to work anymore. Big files are negatives." Another said that a college counselor at the private school that her child attends advised students to "get a job." This could be working at a coffee shop or restaurant to understand the value of low-wage labor, or volunteering as an EMT, a gig that requires arduous and emotionally draining work. Either way, "The sense was, 'Don't go on one of the poverty tours in Peru—get a job. Stop doing all this stuff that rich kids do.'"

Source: "This Year's College Admissions Horror Show" by Nicole Laorte, Town & Country, April 1, 2022

I can remember hanging around the soccer sidelines as my eighth-grade daughter was out there playing on an average team in an average local soccer league. Nobody on the field was going pro.

As I was sharing a snack with some friends and kicking the ball to one of the little brothers on the sideline, here was the dialogue:

Me: I think my daughter may give up soccer after this season.

TigerMom: Oh God. Is everything okay with you guys?

Me: What do you mean?

TigerMom: I have my daughter staying with soccer, even if she hates it.

Me: The kids are in eighth grade. What's the big deal?

TigerMom: Don't you get it? Colleges want to see commitment and consistency in an applicant.

Me: Colleges? I thought they were starting high school next year.

TigerMom: I hope our daughters can still be friends.

On the way home, I asked my wife what just happened.

She said, "Duh, they all thought the college admissions counselors were listening in on the conversation."

"But they were eighth graders running around and enjoying the last months of true childhood," I protested.

"Doesn't matter," said my wife. "You should hang around the school for a week with me when I volunteer to grade papers and see how the parents lie, cheat, and steal to get their kids retested if they got a "C" or a "B" on a test. *Oh, Johnny got home so late from his origami class, he really couldn't prepare for the test. It's not fair to him.*"

In eighth grade.

Chapter 12: Avoiding the Stupidity of Relying on Family and Friends

I will say it again: be careful when relying on advice from family and friends. Learn to listen and be polite in these discussions; for better or worse, they are people who care for you and believe they are helping.

Most of this advice is well-intentioned, but it's based on the small sample of experiences of the loved one. Many times, these experiences are dated or heavily skewed based on factors irrelevant to you.

If Uncle Pete met Aunt Sue at Uptown College and they have been happily married for thirty years, of course they will have fond memories of Uptown. They won't mention that it took five and half years to graduate, thanks to overcrowded classes. That they each changed their course of study three times. Or that they couldn't find jobs for a more than a year after graduation with the crappy majors they were stuck in. They're still huge fans of the football team!

Listen respectfully, but don't be lazy. If you must, find somebody a degree or two removed from your immediate circle. Push for unbiased guidance and turn that person into an objective sounding board. So, dig and do the research and play out the pros and cons, especially when faced with such an emotionally freighted Tectonic Decision.

Section 4: Getting Blinded by the Upside

To know what you know and what you do not know, that is true knowledge.
~ Confucius

Many times, when reaching for a goal, we are blinded to the risks and potential fallout from the decision to "go for it." Sometimes this is done in a calculating manner: If I make that motorcycle jump over the river, I'll be famous. If I miss, I'll still be famous. And sometimes, we just don't think about the downside of taking that risk.

The risks are not always visible or obvious. We may be in a familiar situation and overestimate our abilities and mentally minimize the risks since we have done something many times without a problem. Other times, it may be a new situation and we run into the problem of "we don't know what we don't know."

Think about standing on a stool in the kitchen and reaching for something on the top shelf. You are reaching, and you are off balance. We should remember that when we reach for anything whether physically or emotionally, we are off balance – and problems can happen. Be focused on the upside of your decision but be sure you can identify and live with the downside.

Once our Tectonic Decision is made, the thinking becomes locked into the goal, and we are often blinded to everything else except reaching that goal. This is when problems arise.

Chapter 13: Blinders Are On: The Sinking of the Cargo Ship *El Faro*

In September 2015, *El Faro*, a 791-foot cargo ship, set out on a run from Jacksonville, FL, to San Juan, Puerto Rico. The 1,200-mile trip would take five days each way and the cargo included several hundred shipping containers and cars. For the captain and his crew, this was a routine trip. Two days later, *El Faro* was 15,000 feet below the surface, resting at the bottom of the sea with all thirty-three crew members lost.

There is nothing routine about being on the ocean. Between 2011 and 2021, almost 900 large ships were lost at sea. That's almost two large ships per week. Several of these were lost without a trace: no distress calls made, no wreckage found, nothing.

In the case of *El Faro*, there were detailed records available from the ship's voice recorder as well as some of the ship-to-shore communications. Using these data, the NTSB identified many causes of the sinking, but we will zero in on where we feel the decision-making was flawed and adjustments not made, even in the face of mounting evidence which led to a catastrophic result.

The obvious contributing cause to the *El Faro* loss was the weather. As the ship departed

Jacksonville, Tropical Storm Joaquin was moving north as the ship was heading south.

For an experienced captain and crew, tropical storms and hurricanes were to be treated with respect, but with proper advance notice, could be maneuvered around or through. Large ships are designed to ride out storms at sea. For example, when a hurricane is expected to hit one of its bases, the U.S. Navy sends all its ships out to sea to ride it out, rather than letting them get banged around in the docks.

Before serving two terms as president of the U.S. in the 1950s, Dwight Eisenhower was a five-star general in the army and was the commander of all U.S. forces in Europe. He was responsible for the Allied Forces attacking from the sea and invading the beaches of Normandy, France on what is known as "D-Day." D-Day was the battle in World War II that turned the war in favor of the U.S. and the Allies.

As Eisenhower was leaving office as president, incoming president John F. Kennedy asked him why D-Day went so well for the Allies. Eisenhower's response: "We had better meteorologists than the Germans." An inaccurate weather forecast could have doomed the landing on the beaches and the war could have had a much different outcome.

Not much has changed since D-Day: accurate weather information is mission-critical to any sea-going operation. Weather information was available to the *El Faro* from several sources. The captain preferred the Bon Voyage System (BVS) weather reports, as they were sent to his email. So, *El Faro* was heading south at about twenty-five miles per hour and Joaquin, which was now Hurricane Joaquin, was heading north at fifteen miles per hour. Think of your reduced reaction time in a head-on auto collision. Every second counts.

The problem was that BVS reports, although they contained useful graphics that the captain preferred, were typically six hours behind reports from other sources, the least of which being the Weather Channel. Using the speeds above, in six hours, the ship and the storm would be 240 miles closer to each other. In twelve hours, well, you get the picture on the damage that can be done when relying on stale weather data, not considering other sources of weather information when there were several available, or more importantly slowing down or changing course.

Changing course on a five-day voyage is no big deal when you have enough warning, which *El Faro* did.

Joaquin was already identified as a building storm. Marine experts agree that it would not have been difficult to change course and avoid the storm. Trouble was, such a change would have delayed the ship's arrival, increased the costs of fuel and crew, and been something of a black mark against the captain. (At the time, the captain had a pending application for a promotion.)

As *El Faro* headed closer to the storm, another weather information source sent an urgent message to the bridge of the ship indicating maximum winds from Joaquin were now more than eighty-five miles per hour. It is unclear whether the captain received this message, but around the same time he was heard on the ship's voice recorder as saying that any further course change wasn't warranted "for a 40-knot [46-miles-per-hour] wind."

No way will I be late with this delivery, was his thought.

The captain also indicated his doubts about the functionality of the ship's wind-speed measurement gauge. Confusion was starting to enter the picture, yet the focus stayed on remaining on course and speed and getting to the destination on time.

Nevertheless, the faulty reliance on the BVS data continued to guide the decision-making of an otherwise experienced and successful captain. Some of the crew were accessing Internet sites, tracking the storm, and relaying data to the captain that were timelier and, unfortunately, more accurate than BVS. Things were much worse than the captain had realized because his frame of reference had been distorted by his reliance on the stale BVS data, and he did not factor in credible information from other sources that contradicted BVS.

All this led to a situation of escalating problems for *El Faro*. Delayed weather forecasts and the captain's refusal to observe, collect data, process the situation, and change course all but sealed the fate of the ship and crew. In another set of decisions that did not properly incorporate the downside, course changes suggested by the crew were rejected by the captain. Moreover, the captain's initial call to his company's contact on shore, the Designated Person Ashore (DPA), did not reflect the level of distress facing *El Faro*. It appeared that the captain continued to be focused on the upside of an on-time delivery and was in steadfast denial of the situation.

The primary responsibility of the DPA is to ensure safe operation of the ship. A DPA is a required position in any commercial shipping company and is usually filled by an experienced former captain or senior engineer. The DPA is the critical link from the captain and crew at sea to the company on land. For example, if the captain had an injured crew member that needed a helicopter evacuation to a hospital, the captain would contact the DPA and the DPA would arrange for it to happen.

The captain's initial call to the DPA did not occur until 7:00 a.m., about forty-five minutes before the ship went down. Incredibly, the DPA did not pick up, so the captain left a voice mail:

> *Captain Lawrence? Captain Davidson. Thursday morning, 0700. We have a navigational incident. I'll keep it short. A scuttle popped open on two-deck and we were having some free communication of water go down the three-hold. Have a pretty good list. I want to just touch—contact you verbally here. Everybody's safe, but I want to talk to you.*

Layman's translation: A window popped open, and water was flowing freely into the ship, so much so that the ship was "listing" or leaning over to one side.

No big deal, right? A captain doing the right thing and checking in with the home base to let them know he had a few things going on. But, and this is a big but, the ship had lost power forty-five minutes earlier and was in the middle of more than 130 mile-per-hour winds. Yes, this was a stressful situation, but this was an experienced captain and crew supported by a team on land. Somebody should have been out ahead of this with some structured thinking of what to do in each of the different scenarios. For example, with water freely entering the ship, the ship listing or beginning to roll over, no power, forty-foot seas, and hurricane-force winds, it was time to declare an all-out emergency and forget about the upside of making a cargo delivery on time.

Before the DPA could return the call, the captain called the after-hours service at 7:01 a.m. The tone was a bit different and perhaps in that one-minute interval since he left the voice mail, the enormity of the situation hit the captain:

> *"Oh, man! The clock is ticking! Can I please speak to a Q.I.?"*

[a QI is a Qualified Individual, the same as a DPA]

The first radio broadcast of a distress message was sent about the same time. Less than twenty minutes later, the captain called for a general alarm, the crew gathered on the starboard side of *El Faro*, and abandoned ship. The last recording was at 7:39 a.m.

What went on here and could this disaster have been prevented with less focus on hitting the objective? I think the answer is a resounding "yes."

As a sea captain myself, I know the ocean is beautiful but dangerous and unforgiving. As the person in charge on a boat or ship, my emotional range is fear first, fun second.

Whatever happens out here is my responsibility.

So, it is a mystery to many who have studied the *El Faro* sinking why the captain waited until the last minute to acknowledge he had a serious problem. By this point in the book, you have realized that the entire cascade of errors was driven by a focus on the upside and not taking action to mitigate issues, despite plenty of data indicating a change was needed. This is a sad example of a situation where the decision maker did not even realize the consequences until it cost him and thirty-two others their lives.

Afterword

In the aftermath of the *El Faro* sinking, finger-pointing, and scrambling for cover was a preoccupation of the shipping company and any other entity or person associated with the disaster. Inevitably, much of blame was put on the captain, but he was not the only cause of the sinking. *El Faro* was an old ship with many problems. Former crew that served on *El Faro* described it as a "rust bucket."

But where was Tote, the company that owned *El Faro*? Every commercial ship has a transponder that always broadcasts its location. At Tote headquarters, there should have been people sitting around a mission-control room tracking the location of all its ships. Perhaps Tote was tracking the ship, but the individual(s) on duty did not want to be the cause of the missed delivery. What if the storm was not that bad and just gave *El Faro* a rough ride? What if Joaquin dissipated and fizzled out? So, the captain and not a single person at Tote were interested in thinking through the catastrophic scenario and how to avoid it. Focus stayed on the upside of an on-time delivery.

The *El Faro* story is a reminder that just because a person may have made a bad decision, it does not mean he is a bad person. The captain's "abandon ship" order was given with enough time to allow thirty-one of the thirty-three crew to get off the ship using life rafts and survival suits, although none survived or were ever found.

As the ship was sinking, remaining on the bridge were the captain and a single crew member. The ship rolled on to its side with the bridge flipped sideways. The last crewman was trapped behind equipment at the "bottom" of the now-sideways bridge. On the "top" of the bridge was the captain. The last recorded messages from *El Faro* were of the captain imploring the crewman to reach him and the captain telling the crewman, "I am not leaving you."

Chapter 14: The Downside: Former McKinsey Chairman Raj Gupta

Rajat Gupta had retired as head of McKinsey & Co., the world's top consulting firm, and he sat on the boards of some of the most prestigious companies in the world, including Proctor & Gamble and Goldman Sachs. While at McKinsey, Gupta oversaw the dramatic growth of a global business and was an adviser to presidents, heads of state, titans of industries, and philanthropists. He counted Bill Gates and Bill Clinton among his close friends. Gupta was reported to be worth more than $100 million and to many, was one of the most accomplished and respected individuals on the planet.

It was his decision to make a fifteen-second phone call that erased all of it and put him in jail for two years. By the time he made that phone call, Gupta's thinking was so distorted, he did not understand the downside of his decision to make that call but was instead blinded by the upside.

Gupta's story is an incredible one. He was born into poverty in India, attended the prestigious Indian Institute of Technology (the top college in India), and earned his MBA from Harvard. He joined McKinsey and, twenty years later in 1994, rose to the position of Worldwide Managing Director. He was the leader of the firm. Gupta was a man who came from little and used his intellect and ambition to make it to the top of the business world.

At the height of his visibility and influence, Gupta met Raj Rajaratnam. The two were raising money for the Indian School of Business. Compared with the urbane and sophisticated Gupta, Rajaratnam was a bear. He ran the Galleon hedge fund and spent most of his day eating at his desk on the phone with different sources of information trying to get what traders call an "edge," or the piece of information or insight that will give the trader an advantage in buying or selling stocks or other securities.

As their relationship matured, Gupta would hang around the Galleon offices and eventually entered a series of business transactions with Rajaratnam. In one of the deals, Gupta formed the venture capital firm New Silk Road, and Rajaratnam invested $50 million in it.

While Gupta was wealthy, Rajaratnam was a swashbuckling billionaire who could move around tens of millions of dollars with a phone call. Gupta wanted this life. So many of his close friends and those that relied upon him were super wealthy. Why not him?

Having spent more than a decade in consulting, I have noticed something I call the

Consultant's Paradox. Most high-level consultants like Gupta attended the best schools and scored the best grades. They went on to work at the best firms. The problem for this "elite" group is that at every client company that hires them, the managers and leaders did not go to the best schools and did not score the best grades.

So, after a long day at the company identifying and fixing what are obvious problems to the consultants, the consultants sit around at dinner and talk amongst themselves about the ineptitude of management and how everything was so fixable. By the time dinner is over and the team is on its second or third round of cocktails, the conversation shifts to a discussion of how the inferior CEO, an inferior human to some consultants, has a net worth fifty times more than the consultant and once the project is finished, it will go to one hundred times more. In a perverse way, we can see the frustration on the part of the consultant. There is a good chance the Consultant's Paradox trapped Gupta and drove his behavior.

Inevitably, even if he did not realize it, Gupta was being groomed as an information source by Rajaratnam. Rajaratnam already had a hand-picked network of individuals feeding him information about the finances of different companies, much of which led to illegal insider trading.

Insider trading occurs when an individual uses non-public information to buy or sell publicly traded securities. For example, the CFO of a public company tells you his company will announce a super-large new order his company is about to get. You think the company's stock will go up once the announcement of the order is made, so you hurry home and buy the stock in advance of the announcement. The stock goes up after the announcement and you sell and collect what is known as an "ill-gotten gain." You have broken the law and can be prosecuted and go to jail. This is not an obscure corner of the finance world. There are plenty of examples out there. Go to Google and enter "insider trading scandals" to see what I mean.

During the height of the financial crisis in 2008, everybody was scared. Investment banks like Bear Stearns and Lehman Brothers collapsed and were absorbed by other banks or liquidated. Bank of America did a rescue purchase of Merrill Lynch.

At the time of the 2008 crisis, we are at the point, where Gupta and Rajaratnam are pals. They see each other often, stay at each other's homes, and talk on the phone all the time.

Let's get back to the decision to make that fifteen-second phone call. Gupta sat on the board of Goldman Sachs. Goldman formed the cornerstone of the financial markets. There were few things Goldman did not do. It traded every type of security or commodity, made investments all over the world, and was the go-to lender for much of corporate America and the premier global dealmaker. Given the unstable financial markets of the 2008 financial crisis, Goldman was on shaky ground, just like all other financial institutions during those difficult times. It needed to make a move to shore up confidence in its brand and, by extension, the entire financial system.

Corporate board meetings are typically held quarterly or monthly. In certain circumstances such as a pending acquisition or large lawsuit, a "special" meeting of the board can be called on short notice. The board represents the interests of the shareholders and has a fiduciary duty to behave as such. For example, the board gathers information from expert compensation firms to help set the pay for the CEO, instead of the CEO deciding how to spend the shareholders' money on himself. Board meetings are where the most sensitive of topics are discussed like an acquisition or extraordinary contract. In other words, things that can move a company's stock price.

The board meeting in question was the special meeting of the Goldman Sachs board on September 23, 2008. In that meeting, the board discussed a $5 billion investment from Berkshire Hathaway, a firm controlled by Warren Buffett who is considered to be the greatest investor of the last century. Amid the 2008 financial crisis, a large investment would do much to improve the outside world's confidence in Goldman, but a $5 billion investment from Warren Buffett would be over-the-top good.

At 3:58 p.m. (stock markets closed at 4:00 p.m.) and immediately after the completion of the Goldman board meeting discussing the Buffett investment, Gupta called Rajaratnam, and they spoke for about fifteen seconds. (This was really stupid.) Records show that sixteen seconds after the call, Rajaratnam-controlled Galleon bought a block of Goldman stock just before the markets closed. After the Buffett investment news about Goldman became public and Goldman's stock increased in value, Rajaratnam sold his Goldman shares for more than $800,000 of profits. Not bad for a fifteen-second phone call and an investment holding period measured in hours.

Anybody with an undergraduate degree in business would know that what Gupta did was pass along inside information and that Rajaratnam was certainly going to trade on it. Gupta, if he was thinking clearly, surely would have realized the downside to his decision to make the phone call.

Gupta was so blinded by the upside that he badly misjudged the downside of his decision to make a phone call to a stock trader a few minutes after a critical board meeting. From my own experience as a public-company CEO, when dealing with information from a public company shared in a confidential board meeting, my lawyers routinely instructed me not to speak to people <u>at all</u> until the sensitive information was made public.

Gupta made an emotional decision (*I want to please Rajaratnam and get more for myself*) from a distorted point of view (*Why can't I be super-rich like these other guys?*). Did Gupta knowingly consider the risks when making his decision? Obviously not, because he would have realized the cataclysmic downside far outweighed his vision of the upside.

Afterword

Rajaratnam was convicted of a series of illegal trading activities, including the Goldman trade, that were fed by his mostly illegal network of tipsters. The SEC claimed Galleon made more than $90 million of illicit profits from using inside information. More than $23 million of the total was generated from trades based on information provided by Gupta. Rajaratnam was sent to prison for eleven years.

As the authorities were closing in on Rajaratnam, wire taps recorded additional inside information regarding Proctor & Gamble passed to him by Gupta. Gupta was convicted of several counts of insider trading and served nineteen months in prison – the same prison that housed Rajaratnam.

The downside of the decision to make that fifteen-second phone call extended beyond the ruin of Gupta's reputation. Between SEC fines, penalties, and restitution plus amounts owed to Goldman Sachs for legal fees, much of his net worth is gone. Gupta moved his primary residence to Florida, a state in which the bankruptcy court cannot claim your home. Years after his release from prison, Gupta continued to profess his innocence.

Chapter 15: No Options: Alabama Football and Coach Nick Saban

It was halftime of the 2018 NCAA Football Championship and Alabama was trailing Georgia by a score of 13-0. As the second half started, the Alabama quarterback, Jalen Hurts, was on the bench. Going into the game, Hurts was 26-2 over the previous two seasons, with one of the losses being in the previous year's championship game. The new quarterback to start the second half for Alabama was unknown freshman Tua.

At the game-watching party I attended, people went crazy. What the heck was Alabama coach Nick Saban thinking? How could he throw a freshman out there in the middle of the biggest game of the year? Oh goodness! Now Alabama won't cover the point spread.

So, what was Coach Saban thinking? Let's learn a little about Saban and Alabama football and you will realize the logic used by Saban to take such a risk to go for the upside, despite the obvious downside.

In sixteen seasons as head coach at Alabama from 2006 to 2022, Saban's teams had 194 wins and 27 losses for an astonishing 88% winning percentage. During that time, Alabama had won six national championships and mixed in two undefeated seasons. In other words, an Alabama loss was not something that happened. They always won. Anything short of a national championship is a failed season at Alabama. Alabama football knew only the upside.

Like many things in life, success begets success in college football. If Alabama keeps winning, more of the top high school prospects will want to play there, showcase their talents on the best team in the biggest games, and enhance their chances of getting drafted into the National Football League and earning financial security for their families.

Alabama starts tracking athletes well before they enter high school and has a database of thousands of prospects. A single recruiting day at an Alabama football game (which I have been at) could include 400 high school players and their families with choice seats and field passes. All this to land a few dozen incoming freshmen each year. On the other end of things, it has been common for half or more of Alabama's twenty-two starting players to be drafted into the NFL each year.

In order to get a sense of how competitive it is to get on the field at a place like Alabama, let me tell a story where I have some personal connection. A relative of mine was being inducted into the University of Florida Sports Hall of Fame and I was in the audience. Florida has won national championships in football, just not as many as Alabama.

One of the inductees was Errict Rhett, a University of Florida running back who went on to play seven seasons in the NFL. He was an accomplished player in the NFL, but what about his time at the University of Florida? Like all heavily recruited scholarship players at top schools, Rhett was a superstar in high school. As he told the story during his acceptance speech, he landed at the University of Florida on a defensive scholarship, but his heart was on offense. And why not? He had just finished running people over and scoring touchdowns at will in high school while being a great defensive player and two-time state wrestling champion.

Rhett was persistent about wanting to be a running back and the coaches finally relented and made him one. The next day at practice, Rhett was listed as the number six running back on the depth chart. (Massive laughter from the audience.) He needed to prove he was better than five other players just to get on the field in a game. Well, over the course of a season, he made it all the way to the number two spot on the chart. He was elated. The only problem was that the number one running back was a guy named Emmett Smith. Smith held all the running records at Florida and went on to become the leading rusher in NFL history. Rhett stuck it out until Smith left for the pros. Rhett then reset all the Florida rushing records and went on to his NFL career. Nothing is easy, especially in college football.

Like Rhett and Emmett Smith, Hurts was a winner. He was a powerlifter growing up and had the unusual combination of arm strength and foot speed that made him difficult to defend. He could beat you with his passing and just as easily break off a run where he would bulldoze defensive players out of the way or simply outrun them.

In his first season as a starter at Alabama, Hurts led the team to a 13-1 record, before losing the national championship by the thinnest of margins to a miracle comeback by Georgia. That season included eleven straight wins at one point. In his second season, he again led the team to a 13-1 record when they entered the championship.

So, how could Coach Saban pull Hurts at halftime? Despite all the success the team and Hurts had going into the game, Alabama was trailing at halftime and was ineffective on offense, barely recording positive yardage in the half. Time for a huge, but calculated risk: all part of being blinded by the upside.

Tua came in to start the second half and led the team to one of the most amazing high-stakes comebacks in all of sports. Highlights included a last-minute touchdown pass to seal the victory.

Did Saban know Tua was capable of such things? Only Saban knows whether this is true but go back to the example of Errict Rhett at Florida. If Tua was able to fight his way into the number two quarterback slot as a freshman, we know he was good. He had to climb his way up from the bottom of the class. And remember, just to get on the team at Alabama, you had to be an all-world high school quarterback. So, Tua faced incredible competition, like Rhett, to make it to the number two quarterback position. Did Alabama and Tua get a little lucky in that second half? Sure, but that's sports.

Saban was losing the biggest game on the biggest stage, and he made the decision that he would do whatever it took to win, even if it meant benching his star quarterback in favor of an unknown freshman.

Saban had a massive database to use in his decision. He coached Tua every day in practice and knew what he could do. Saban was also wiling to live with the consequences and worst-case outcomes of his decision. It would have been easy to leave Hurts in the game and if Alabama lost, there would be little criticism of Hurts, Saban, or Alabama football beyond what a great game Georgia had played and how they had bottled up the Alabama offense.

Saban understood the downside of "going for it." If Alabama lost, Saban would never be forgiven for pulling Hurts. Forget about the wins and national championship trophies in the Alabama athletic center. He would have been run out of town and into a witness-protection program.

But he didn't care since he had made his unemotional decision and was willing to live with the downside. Saban had an accurate factual base for his decision: Hurts was having a bad game, Alabama was losing, and he had Tua ready to go. Of course, Saban wanted the upside of a win, but more importantly, he understood and was willing to accept the downside of his decision.

Afterword

The year after the dramatic Tua-led Alabama win in the 2018 National Championship, Tua was named the starting quarterback and Hurts was the backup. To advance to the playoffs and have a shot at back-to-back national championships, the 12-0 Alabama team needed to beat Georgia in the SEC championship game. Midway through the game, with Alabama trailing, Tua went down with an injury. What happened next? You guessed it, Hurts came in and led Alabama to a wild come-from-behind victory and a spot in the playoff.

The next year Hurts left Alabama and played his final college year at Oklahoma, another perennial college football powerhouse. He broke several school records and posted a 12-2 record, which included a loss in the playoff semifinals. A win in that semifinal playoff game would have set up an Alabama vs Oklahoma and Tua vs Hurts National Championship game.

Both Tua and Hurts went on to successful NFL careers. Hurts and his Philadelphia Eagles had the best record in the NFL in 2022 and lost in the Super Bowl by a field goal. He subsequently signed one of the largest contracts in NFL history. In July 2024, Tua signed the largest contract for a quarterback in the history of the Miami Dolphins football team.

After the departures of Tua and Hurts, Saban added his sixth national championship a year later and then announced his retirement in January 2024.

Chapter 16: Avoiding the Stupidity of Being Blinded By the Upside

Being blinded by the upside is an easy way to make a foolish decision. Sometimes the allure of winning that game or getting *El Faro* to its destination port on schedule blinds us to everything else. We talk ourselves into the decision since the upside is so big. But, more often than not, the upside is illusory. Think of it like a lottery ticket: for $5, you have a chance to win $5 million. In 99.99 percent of the cases, you will not win the $5 million; you will win nothing. Unless you have an edge in making your decision, like Nick Saban and Alabama football, that reduces your downside risk, avoid the lottery mindset, and do not get blinded by the upside.

Ironically, it takes a fair degree of intelligence to assess the upside of a decision. When there are significant stakes involved, like the thirty-three lives lost on *El Faro*, there are almost always decision-makers involved that knowingly calculate the upside.

If we get this delivery into port on time with these storms, I will become one of the go-to captains at my company.

This is the kind of justification that goes on in our heads when we are blinded.

The second concept from this chapter is to properly consider the downside of a decision. Saban knew what he was doing and was willing to accept the risks. While it may have appeared to be a desperate, impulsive decision by Saban to pull Hurts in favor of an untested freshman, it was nothing of the sort. More so than most, Saban is a public figure and everything he says, he eats, and he wears is scrutinized.

Because of this, he knew that his decision to pull Hurts would be analyzed by every sports reporter and television analyst for the rest of his life. Did Saban feel he could withstand the downside of going for it? Given his record and his relationship with the media, I think so, but nothing is certain about this other than Saban's record of accomplishment to that point in time, earning him something of a safety net if things had gone wrong. Make sure you have a safety net if you reach for the upside.

But how could Gupta, a titan of the industry, sit in a board meeting, learn of super-sensitive information, and then rush to the phone and call a trader? Even if he and Rajaratnam were discussing tickets to the Notre Dame football game for the upcoming weekend, it was a massive screw up to place the call. Hasn't he ever watched a television show or movie where the police pull the cell phone records? If he was thinking in a deliberate and calculating manner, he would have considered the downside, going to jail for insider trading, and never placed that call. Gupta was blinded by the upside, reacted impulsively, and unknowingly made a Tectonic Decision that ruined his life in fifteen seconds.

Section 5: Trusting the Media

The media is the right arm of anarchy.
~ Dan Brown

Daniel J. Boorstin was the author of *The Image: A Guide to Pseudo-Events in America*. A pseudo-event is a man-made construct. Boorstin coined the term for things like "grand openings" and "press conferences." If news was meant to be reported, why create an event (or more properly, a pseudo-event) by inviting people to a hotel conference room, offering food and drink, and engaging in discussion about the "news" being released?

Boorstin had another killer concept in *The Image*. We have evolved from a society that admired people for their accomplishments (e.g., explorers and scientists) to one that admires people simply because they are well-known (e.g., a celebrity). He coined the term "well-knownness." For the most part, celebrities are known for their well-knownness, not for achievements or contributions to society.

From *The Image*:

"We can fabricate fame, we can at will (though usually at considerable expense) make a man or a woman well known; but we cannot make him or her great. In a now almost forgotten sense, all heroes are self-made...

The hero was distinguished by his achievement, the celebrity by his image or trademark. The hero created himself; the celebrity is created by the media. The hero was a big man; the celebrity is a big name...

Boorstin wrote this more than sixty years ago.

Almost everything Boorstin has to say in *The Image* is applicable to today's world of celebrity-journalists and why determining the truth is so distorted. We live in a world in which a TMZ reporter telling us about what a television personality was wearing in the airport earns more than the heart surgeon who literally holds life in her hands every day. The Kardashians are famously famous – as many have quipped – for being famous.

Over the last few decades, the news media have morphed into entertainment companies, and the entertainment they sell is conflict and confrontation. Those who own or control the media are on a full-time quest to push their own interests or, obviously, push for ratings. The facts and the truth are important, but not central to these goals. Sometimes reporting incorrect information (usually sensational) keeps a story alive when the reporter or journalist gets to do a *mea culpa* and make herself part of the story.

The reporter remaining objective and staying out of the story once was one of the guiding principles of journalism. Not anymore. In the 1970s, Tom Wolfe and Hunter S. Thompson introduced the world to "new journalism," originally a fringe movement that placed the writer in the middle of the story and made it, ultimately, about him or her. That kind of reporting has since become the norm, and the "celebrity-journalist" is a new and growing category. They get the ratings and the big paychecks for creating controversy, stirring things up, and distorting the view of the truth. It is almost impossible to distinguish between entertainment and news today.

A few stats from Louis Menand in *The New Yorker* magazine sum up the problem:

> Back in 1976, even after Vietnam and Watergate, 72 percent of the public said they trusted the news media. Today, the figure is 34 percent. Among Republicans, it's 14 percent.

Chapter 17: For Real? Journalists Who Were Spies for the CIA

It may appear that the celebrity-journalist is a new phenomenon that is a creature of the explosion of the media industry since the Internet went mainstream. In fact, it is quite an old concept.

> In 1953, Joseph Alsop, then one of America's leading syndicated columnists, went to the Philippines to cover an election. He did not go because he was asked to do so by his syndicate. He did not go because he was asked to do so by the newspapers that printed his column. He went at the request of the CIA.

This passage is from "The CIA and the Media" written by Carl Bernstein and published in *Rolling Stone* magazine in 1977. By then, this had already amounted to more than twenty-five years of the media acting as spies for the CIA. Bernstein's research said that more than 400 journalists had carried out assignments on behalf of the CIA while they were in foreign countries.

We are not talking about scrappy, second-tier media organizations trying to break into the club. Bernstein points out that the CIA said its best information came from journalists at *The New York*

Times, CBS, and *Time Inc.*, three of the most respected media corporations of the era.

Defenders of the journalist-as-a-spy approach say that they were just doing their duty as U.S. citizens to help protect the country. The CIA says that foreign correspondents were well-positioned "assets" since they were afforded greater freedoms and access than most U.S. citizens. That access included such things as meetings with government officials and displays of new military capabilities.

The evidence from Bernstein's story suggests a formal relationship, rather than a, "Hey, tell us what you saw over there," approach.

> In the 1950s, it was not uncommon for returning reporters to be met at the ship by CIA officers. "There would be these guys from the CIA flashing ID cards and looking like they belonged at the Yale Club," said Hugh Morrow, a former *Saturday Evening Post* correspondent who is now press secretary to former Vice President Nelson Rockefeller. "It got to be so routine that you felt a little miffed if you weren't asked."

In many ways, the journalist-spy of the latter half of the twentieth century was more hero than celebrity in Boorstin's model. The journalist-spy took risks, was working for the greater good, and was often unpaid. To this day, the CIA has kept the names of the journalists secret. While the practice of using journalists as CIA assets distorts the concept of an objective newsroom, it is understandable why the model was in place and not debatable that it produced value to the U.S. without generating fame and fortune for the journalist.

Chapter 18: Talking Heads: Former Military Officials as Television Analysts, Paid by the Pentagon

Paul Vallely was a graduate of West Point and served in the army for more than thirty years. He was a Ranger and a decorated soldier who served in Vietnam. He retired a few ticks from the top as a Major General and the Deputy Commander of the Pacific, certainly a Boorstin hero, if there ever was one. He was also a "force multiplier."

According to the Department of Defense, a force multiplier is:

> A capability that when added to and employed by a combat force significantly increases the combat potential of that force and thus enhances the probability of mission accomplishment.

How can one solider, even one as accomplished as Vallely, be considered a force multiplier? In this case, Vallely did not have expensive equipment or specially trained troops. The Pentagon referred to Vallely as a force multiplier because of his vocal cords.

Vallely, like many other former senior military officers, was often on television and other media to provide expert commentary to the audiences. After all, these analysts had long, and distinguished military careers and many times would make a visit to war-torn hot spot to add authenticity to his comments.

In "Message Machine: Behind TV's Analysts, the Pentagon's Hidden Hand," an exhaustive piece on the subject in *The New York Times* written by David Barstow in 2008, we learn that unbeknownst to viewers, and many times to the media networks, these analysts were being briefed and paid by the Pentagon. Further, many analysts had direct ties to military contractors that were bidding for billions of dollars in Pentagon business, especially during wartime.

Barstow describes the access the analysts were granted as part of the program and how such access is valuable if the analyst is also working for a contractor trying to do business with the Pentagon. Regular briefings, talking points, and emergency demands for op-ed articles when there was criticism of the Pentagon were all in a day's work for the seventy-five former military commanders who were now paid talking heads for the Pentagon.

One of the phrases often associated with winning a military conflict is the need to "win the hearts and minds" of the country's population. For example, if our military can convince the population of a communist country that life will be better for them under a U.S.-supported non-communist government, perhaps they will lay down their arms or not resist the objectives of the U.S.

Central to winning this part of a battle are Psychological Operations or PSYOPs. In a PSYOP, the military executes a series of actions to influence the population. Actions include the dissemination of information pamphlets, media appearances, social media influencing, and humanitarian evacuations of non-combatants.

All of this is done to sway public opinion in favor of U.S. military objectives. It's not much different than a branding and promotional campaign for a new type of soft drink or disposal diaper. It's all about messaging to the audience to move them in a direction. And in this case, the PSYOP was being performed not on the population of a war-torn country, but on the U.S. television audience to help the Pentagon build support for its actions. Tellingly, Vallely was a PSYOPs expert.

As a viewer of the military analysts, we are really stuck with understanding how to trust anybody for decision-making about wartime topics. Imagine the following:

> Bossman: Hey, did you see General Zod on CNN last night? They don't come much more accomplished and well-spoken than him.

CubicleGuy: You watch that stuff?

Bossman: These guys were there, in the battles, and fighting for our country. They know what they're talking about.

CubicleGuy: Yeah, I get it, but Zod retired from the military like fifteen years ago. His last war was Vietnam in the 1960s. What does he know about present-day Iraq and Afghanistan? Did he ever fly a drone?

Once again, CubicleGuy asks the right questions to set the proper context for what to believe in the media.

Barstow further describes the depth and breadth of the analyst program:

> The Pentagon paid a private contractor, Omnitec Solutions, hundreds of thousands of dollars to scour databases for any trace of the analysts, be it a segment on "The O'Reilly Factor" or an interview with *The Daily Inter Lake* in Montana (circulation 20,000). Omnitec evaluated their appearances using the same tools as corporate branding experts.

And then there is Secretary of Defense Donald Rumsfeld talking about the war in Iraq with his assistant, Ms. Clarke.

From Barstow's article:

On April 12, 2003, with major combat almost over, Mr. Rumsfeld drafted a memorandum to Ms. Clarke. "Let's think about having some of the folks who did such a good job as talking heads in after this thing is over," he wrote.

This all leaves us in a place of deep skepticism. How can we believe anything we hear or see in the media? When Boorstin-certified heroes like Vallely go to the dark side and become celebrities, there is little hope that the current media-industrial complex can help us with gaining traction for an understanding of the world.

Chapter 19: A Million Little Lies: The Story of James Frey and Oprah

Contrast the journalist-spy approach with that of James Frey. Frey is the author of *A Million Little Pieces*, a memoir. The book detailed Frey's experiences with alcohol and drug addiction, as well as his life of crime. He shows up at home one day in his early twenties and is such a mess, his parents check him into a detox and rehabilitation clinic. Most of the book describes Frey's time in rehab and his subsequent time in prison, in graphic detail.

The book did not do much when it was first published, but that changed when Frey caught lightning in a bottle: Oprah Winfrey added it to Oprah's Book Club and had Frey as a guest on her show. Sales of the book took off and it was on top of best-seller lists for months. Oprah teared up as she spoke with Frey on her show. Millions purchased the book. Movie deals were in the works. Frey was a star.

Frey was also a liar. After his appearance on *Oprah*, the website The Smoking Gun website did some fact-checking of arrest records, hospitalizations, and other salacious details in the book. Many facets of the story did not check out and the website challenged him. Soon thereafter, Frey and his publisher, Random House, had to admit that the book was not the truthful memoir it had originally been marketed to be. It was a fabrication based on *some* of the facts of Frey's life.

Frey had to go back on *Oprah* to explain himself. Oprah was pissed. She extracted confessions from Frey and his publisher of the falsified nature of the story. Readers were allowed to return the book for a full refund from Random House and all future copies had author's and publisher's notes informing readers that the book was a work of fiction. Ironically, when Frey had first pitched a version of the book as a novel, no publishing house would take it.

Other than making millions and becoming a household name from his fabricated story, what happened to Frey? After Random House kicked him out, *A Million Little Pieces* was made into a movie and his next book (yes, a novel this time) was immediately picked up by another publisher. Frey's profile only grew.

Using the Boorstin formula, Frey was no hero, but he was certainly a celebrity. As if telling truth from fiction was not hard enough, we have celebrity-journalists like Frey distorting and flat-out lying about the story.

Chapter 20: Avoiding the Stupidity of Trusting the Media

In a world of 500 channels on television and an endless number of websites spewing data and opinions, where can we start this analysis? Let's start with sports. As a society, we seem to have an insatiable appetite for sports and sports news. Since its debut in 1979, ESPN has become the dominant source of sports information and, more than forty years later, it is everywhere—on your computer, phone, television, airplane seat, etc. But why is ESPN (and its competitors) so popular? A simple answer: it is reliable.

Sports information, with few exceptions, is based on hard facts: batting averages, shooting percentages, tackles made, goals scored, and on the list goes. There is no debate about the facts; the stats are the stats, and they are verifiable and rarely in dispute. There is no interpretation or analysis involved. Either you won or you lost, you made the shot, or you didn't. ESPN and others pile on loads of opinions and analyses, but this is the dessert to the meat and potatoes dinner of the hard data.

Contrast sports information in the media with our generals reporting on how we are doing against enemies in other countries, and the comparison is a joke. We can only rely on the expert's opinion or homemade scorecard for how things are going in a war zone.

"U.S. troops drove back the enemy and took possession of a strategic mountain pass in Afghanistan last night."

I don't know about you, but I don't see a frame of reference here. Nobody is telling us there are twelve key mountain passes and if we control all of them, we choke off the enemy supply lines. Even knowing that, does it really help us decide if we are winning or losing? Basketball scores are up on the screen and change with every basket, so it's easy to tell how things are going.

And what about outright fabrications by people like James Frey? We first must realize that there is no professional licensing test to become a journalist or an author. Anybody can do it (present company included). Frey is a perfect example of everything that is wrong with the media and how right Boorstin was about celebrities replacing heroes in today's world. Hey, if you get a lot of "likes" or page views, it must be awesome, and it must be true. Trouble is that these fabrications get repeated over and over as they are picked up by other media outlets and rebroadcast to still more people. After a short incubation, the fabrications become the truths that people repeat to each other. Stupid.

Same for our respected military officers who have become shills for the Pentagon.

To me, it's an embarrassment that men and women who have sacrificed so much and defended our country are peddling marketing pitches for a few extra dollars. Such individuals should be beyond reproach.

How about this: let's fix the military pension system to avoid these temptations.

Section 6: Using Quick and Dirty Thinking

A half-truth is more dangerous than a lie.
~ Benjamin Franklin

We all use quick and dirty thinking because it is easy and satisfying. A quick solution appeals to our sense of immediate gratification. But, with few exceptions, quick and dirty thinking creates a false sense of truth and can be outright dangerous, especially when a Tectonic Decision is at hand.

Think about the following the next time somebody suggests a quick and dirty solution: A few synonyms for "quick and dirty" from PowerThesarus.org:

- Makeshift
- Off-the-Cuff
- Kludge
- Band-aid

You get the idea.

I had a friend who told me about his experience in law school. For a three-hour final exam essay, he was taught to spend at least two hours outlining and putting together the facts. Then, with thirty to sixty minutes left on the exam clock, he would write the essay. This "think first, then act" model has far greater applicability than we realize and, if you can do it, will lead you on the path away from quick and dirty thinking.

Chapter 21: You're Not So Smart: Misguided Use of Rules of Thumb

Herbert Simon was a Ph.D. economist who is credited with creating the concept of a heuristic in the 1950s. The word "heuristic" is derived from a Greek word meaning "to discover." A heuristic is a problem-solving strategy or method that uses a practical approach to find a solution. It is a rule of thumb or a simplified approach to solving a problem, rather than using a systematic or algorithmic method.

Our brain utilizes heuristics to estimate things and drive behavior. For example, deciding who will win the election in your county based on the lawn signs in your neighborhood, voting "innocent" as a juror because the defendant is well-dressed, or avoiding air travel out of fear of harm, even though you are two thousand times more likely to die in an automobile accident than a plane crash.

Heuristics are everywhere, and we all use them. Daniel Kahneman was a Nobel-prize winning behavioral economist who built on the work of Simon in this area. In his best-selling book *Thinking, Fast and Slow*, Kahneman describes two types of thinking that happen inside our brains:

System 1: Quick decision-making, often driven by emotion and heuristics

System 2: Deliberate decision-making, driven by logic and algorithms

When we talk about avoiding bad decisions, we want to avoid heuristics and avoid System 1 thinking. But why? There are volumes written about how heuristics introduce bias into decision-making. Take the following example of a biased decision made based on a heuristic:

> JuniorGirl: Where do you think I should go to college?
>
> TigerMom: Your dad and I both went to Uptown College, and we have good jobs, two cars in the driveway, and are loving parents.
>
> JuniorGirl: Thanks, Mom. That makes it easy for me. If it's good enough for you guys, it's good enough for me.

JuniorGirl accessed her System 1 thinking, used a simple heuristic – if it's good enough for Mom, it means it's good enough for me, and made a decision.

Ouch! A Tectonic Decision heading for stupidity – a decision that will affect the arc of her entire life. Perhaps there is a better way:

JuniorGirl: Where do you think I should go to college?

TigerMom: Your dad and I both went to Uptown College, and we have good jobs, two cars in the driveway, and are loving parents.

JuniorGirl: Okay, I will include Uptown on my list of possibilities.

TigerMom: What? What are you talking about?

JuniorGirl: I did some research and learned that I should apply to at least a half dozen colleges and should match up my interests and strengths with the offerings of the school. Additionally, I need to understand the data on graduation rates and what percentage of graduates get jobs today or go on to graduate school.

No heuristic being used here. Instead, a rigorous System 2 thinking process is in action and is fully engaged. You may say, "What do you have against heuristics and System 1 thinking?" Plenty, especially when it comes to preparing for Tectonic Decisions because heuristics invite bias into the process and **bias is the Black Death of decision-making**.

We develop biases based on our experiences. If our experience with teenagers working behind the counter at McDonalds has been unpleasant, we may develop a bias and assume most or all teenagers are unpleasant as waiters, parking-lot attendants, etc.

In the example above, TigerMom is pushing a bias-driven decision through System 1 emotional brain thinking. TigerMom is making an emotionally motivated decision based on a heuristic. "I turned out fine and I went to Uptown so JuniorGirl should do the same."

As was discussed previously, don't take the advice of family when it comes to Tectonic Decisions. Listen and consider the advice, but most advice from family is driven by System 1 emotional brain thinking and is heavily biased.

If there is one consistent point across all chapters in this book, it is the following:

Do everything possible to avoid bias entering the process for a decision. Without bias, your chances of making a good decision increase dramatically.

But how do we clear away bias in the decision-making process? Let's start with "How to Root Out Bias from Your Decision-Making Process" by Thomas C. Redman in the Harvard Business Review in 2017:

> Making good decisions involves hard work. Important decisions are made in the face of great uncertainty, and often under time pressure. The world is a complex place: People and organizations respond to any decision, working together or against one another, in ways that defy comprehension. There are too many factors to consider. There is rarely an abundance of relevant, trusted data that bears directly on the matter at hand. Quite the contrary, there are plenty of partially relevant facts from disparate sources — some of which can be trusted, some not — pointing in different directions.

Redman goes on to describe how we have the tendency to make a decision, then go back and assemble supporting data. It's just faster and easier this way. The problem is that we all have built-in biases, and we need to recognize this when faced with an important decision like applying to college. The hard part here is that each of us as individuals is poorly qualified to make most Tectonic Decisions.

For example, if you have a heart condition, you're not the person making the Tectonic Decision about what medicines you should take. Remember, a Tectonic Decision is one that is important, but infrequent, which usually means it can affect the trajectory of your life. It would be too big of a decision for you to select the medicines, so you rely on a cardiologist since, several times per day, the cardiologist makes medicine selections for people with heart conditions. The decision for the cardiologist is important, but not infrequent, so to the cardiologist, it is not Tectonic.

This should move us toward setting a rule for decisions and avoiding the stupidity of quick and dirty thinking:

> If it feels like you are making a Tectonic Decision, stop. Step back and engage System 2 thinking by gathering data and expert opinions to formulate the correct approach to the decision-making process.

Chapter 22: Why Can't I Lose Ten Pounds?

"I really need to get back in shape." How many times have you heard this or said it yourself? What does this statement really mean? And how big of a problem is this?

Rosalie Bradford was five feet six inches tall and weighed 1,200 pounds. She was essentially immobile and bed-ridden for more than eight years. At one point, she was more than eight feet wide. Two beds were chained together to support her weight. It took her ninety minutes to take a bath. Bradford attempted suicide by taking an overdose of sleeping pills. Her weight and size nullified the effect of the overdose. She only slept for two days.

Bradford lost more than 900 pounds, which at the time, was recognized by the Guinness Book of World Records as the biggest weight loss ever by a woman. Her first efforts at exercise consisted of clapping her hands while watching an exercise video. She made the decision to stop being lazy physically and mentally and recognized there was no shortcut to weight loss.

After losing the weight, Bradford went on to be a motivational and inspirational speaker. It is instructive to take a quote from one of Bradford's speeches on how to lose weight:

"Start where you are and chisel away."

Another fitness all-star who did not use quick and dirty thinking was a former medical student in Great Britain. He was a gifted athlete who specialized in the one-mile run. But all elite runners are gifted, so how could he distinguish himself and go faster, especially since, as a medical student, he had only forty-five minutes per day to train?

The student surmised that he could run a faster mile if he ran at a steady pace on each of the four laps around the track that constitute the one-mile race, rather than conserving energy in the early laps and then sprinting all-out near the end. In other words, he had a well-thought-out theory about how to improve and he was able to test it.

Kahneman System 2 thinking at its elegant best.

During his break each day, he and a few colleagues would go out to the track to run a series of quarter-mile, one-lap intervals and try to run consistent and repeatable times on each lap before they hurried back into class.

The student was not hooked up to any machines to measure his VO2 max, respiration rate, and heart rate. There was no Apple Watch. There was no high-protein keto vegan low-carb South

Beach specialized diet. He just went out and ran and relied on his theory about consistent lap times. He was not quick and dirty in his thinking, but quite scientific about it.

On May 6, 1954, Roger Bannister became the first man ever to run a sub-four-minute mile.

So, when you hear somebody (or yourself) say, "I am going to lose ten pounds," think about Bradford and think about Bannister. Bradford had to start slowly and work her way toward a goal. Bannister was already in elite company but needed to figure out how to do better. Both attacked the problems they faced by avoiding quick and dirty thinking.

Back to your weight-loss problem.

A better approach might be something like, "Well, two years ago, I weighed 150 pounds, and today I weigh 167 pounds. I want to weigh 150 pounds again." So, you need to lose seventeen pounds, not ten. Why bother setting a random objective to lose ten pounds when the real goal should be to lose seventeen pounds?

Am I really seventeen pounds overweight? This question falls into the same category as:

- Is my business losing *that* much money?
- Is my child that bad at math?
- Am I studying ten hours per week, and it should be twenty?

We all get embarrassed by something at some point in time. Should you let that rush of emotion dictate your path? Absolutely not. Am I lying to myself when I say I need to lose ten pounds? No, but am I using quick and dirty thinking? Yes. Be honest and scientific about losing weight. Admit how bad it is now and use that as your true starting point. It worked for Bradford, and I doubt you need to lose 900 pounds.

Toughen up, take the pain upfront, and admit how big the problem is. As the expression goes, "The truth will set you free," but it also can depress you.

Cheer up. It's not where you start, it's where you finish. The lesson here is that if you want to, or dare to, be precise about your fitness journey. Be scientific about it and don't go for the quick and dirty "gotta lose ten pounds approach." There are better ways.

Of all the quick and dirty methods we are exposed to, weight-loss scams are among the most prevalent. There are books, websites, newsletters, and television and radio shows, etc., and it seems that people cannot stop talking about intermittent fasting, the juice cleanse, weight-loss pills, and the list goes on. This is a multi-billion industry built on our penchant for a quick and dirty answer.

From the FDA website:

> It would be nice if you could lose weight simply by taking a pill, wearing a patch, or rubbing in a cream, but claims that you can lose weight without changing your habits just aren't true. And some of these products could even hurt your health. Learn to recognize false claims in weight loss ads and false online stories about weight loss products….Permanent weight loss requires permanent lifestyle changes, so don't trust any product that promises once-and-for-all results.

In other words, the FDA is saying that if you want to lose weight, don't be quick and dirty about it.

We can write an entire book about these scams, but let's focus on Sensa, which was one of the most heavily advertised products in recent years and is representative of the falsehoods perpetuated by the weight-loss "industry." The Sensa claim was that all you needed to do was sprinkle a little bit on your food to lose weight. Salt, pepper, and a little Sensa. Got it.

From a Sensa news release:

> Based on more than twenty years of his research linking human olfactory senses to appetite and overeating, Dr. Alan Hirsch developed the SENSA® Weight-Loss System. SENSA® consists of patent pending blends of scented Tastants that you sprinkle on food that are designed to stimulate the olfactory senses and trigger satiety.

> Sensa said that its crystals or "Tastants," once added to food and eaten, promoted feelings of fullness.

> Really? Like many of the weight-loss scams, Sensa relied on the propensity for people to go for the quick fix. The "science" behind Sensa was created by Hirsch, a physician who also owned the Smell and Taste Treatment Research Foundation.

> The foundation performed all the "testing" that helped Sensa claim that you can eat as much of anything you like, as long as you sprinkle Sensa on the food. Claims were for thirty pounds of weight loss within six months.

> Hirsch even claimed to have a study that was peer-reviewed by an endocrinology association to

support his claims. Such a study never existed, and the company was skewered on ABC's 20/20 news television show. Despite all of this, Sensa sold more than $350 million of products over a five-year period before it started to unravel.

The first big lawsuit was in California for false advertising. Sensa paid $900,000 in 2013. In 2014, the hammer dropped and the FTC fined Sensa for $26.4 million, which the FTC distributed to almost 500,000 Sensa customers. Soon thereafter, Sensa was liquidated.

If you re-read the paragraphs above, you can swap in a few words and numbers, and everything here can apply to the thousands of weight-loss scams that have appealed to our lust for quick results. Some of my historical favorites include those vibrating belts that "smooth" your skin, the special sunglasses that make everything a bit duller to reduce temptation to reach for the fancy packaging of some foods and, finally, the tape worm: just eat a few every day and the pounds will drip away. Stupid.

Given continued proliferation of these scams, it seems we are all getting dumber. Or, more plausibly in a world of texting and instant messages, we are simply succumbing to speed and all the mistakes that come with it. Instead of using our brains and thinking through problems, we keep going for the immediate gratification of the quick and dirty solution.

Chapter 23: Turn the Tables: Managing a High-Stakes Interview

"We just don't think you're a match for the position." Not the words you ever want to hear, especially if it's a job you really want. You polished up the resume, got a new dress and shoes – you were ready for this interview. Why did it fail? There could be many reasons, but avoiding a quick and dirty approach would improve your odds.

Thomas Edison added the "soup test" to his interviews. While Edison was interviewing a group of potential research assistants over lunch, he ordered soup for the table. If an interviewee added salt and/or pepper to the soup before tasting it, it was a tell for Edison. Edison did not want to hire people who made assumptions; he wanted things measured and evaluated scientifically. If you put salt and pepper in your soup before tasting it, you were making an assumption about how the soup might taste. Not cool for Edison.

For the Edison test, pay attention to the question, gesture, or action of the interviewer. Are you in a formal one-on-one situation? A group interview? A casual setting? What are they really asking you or, more importantly, trying to find out about you? Interviews are the last place for quick and dirty thinking.

Another method that is gaining traction in the interview world is a bit more scientific than Edison's soup test. Asymmetric Information Management (AIM) seeks to separate those that are telling the truth from those who are embellishing or flat-out lying. The AIM method of lie-detection has been championed by Cody Porter. He summarizes it as follows:

> "Specifically, interviewers make it clear to interviewees that if they provide longer, more detailed statements about the event of interest, then the investigator will be better able to detect if they are telling the truth or lying," Porter said. "For truth-tellers, this is good news. For liars, this is less good news."
>
> Source: "Lie-detection by strategy manipulation: Developing an asymmetric information management (AIM) technique, Porter, et al, Applied Research in Memory and Cognition, January 2020

In a controlled test by Porter, two groups of people were sent to do a project. Upon their return, each person sat for an interview about the project. Half the group was told to answer all questions truthfully and with as much detail as possible, while the other half was told to withhold information about the project and lie to create a story about doing something else.

Remarkably, the AIM method identified those telling the truth 81 percent of the time.

As an interviewee, you may not realize the AIM method is being used on you. The trouble is that we are taught that "less is more" when answering questions, especially in an interview. The trick is how to determine when to prove you are a truth-teller. There is nothing wrong with saying, "I know I answered your question, but there is a bit more I want to add to color in my response."

I once interviewed a quiet and soft-spoken young woman (let's call her Sally). I asked her to tell me something unusual that has happened to her recently. Sally proceeded in her pleasant monotone to describe how she and some friends were almost lost at sea when the mast on their sailboat snapped off, the boat capsized, and they spent the night clinging to the hull until help arrived the next day. Yeah, she was a truth-teller. Sally had command of the details and explained everything. After we verified her story, Sally was hired.

In another example, I had a friend who did not respond to the prompt for his college essay applications. In his words, "I really wasn't much of a writer when I was in high school." How did he turn the tables and avoid quick and dirty thinking? He drew pictures. While he may not have been confident in his writing skills at that time, he was an accomplished artist. He told the story of his life and answered the essay questions with a series of drawings. He was granted admission and attended the college.

But the story doesn't end there. He went on to be a hugely successful professional and lifelong supporter of the school.

What did the school do? It changed its application to add language similar to the following:

> If there are other materials you feel should be submitted with your application so the school can get a more complete understanding of your strength as an applicant, please include. Such materials may include drawings, recordings, videos, or any other materials you deem appropriate.

I never did ask him how he handled his first job interview; but, given the level of preparation, creativity, and initiative he demonstrated on his college application, I may talk to him about his job interviews and turn that into another book. This guy knew how to avoid quick and dirty thinking and turn the tables.

It is always smart to do your homework before a job interview. There are many things you can do to prepare. One of them is **not** scanning the company's website so you can parrot back company lingo. That would be quick and dirty.

What should you do?

For example, if you are interviewing at a technology firm, go back and learn about a company from the 1950s called Shockley Semiconductor. Shockley was one of the first businesses in Silicon Valley. It made, well, semiconductors (materials made of silicon that form the brains of a computer).

Shockley and two of his colleagues were awarded Nobel Prizes in the 1950s for their groundbreaking work in this area.

You say, "Dude, so what. The tech company I want to work for makes enterprise software."

Well, eight senior engineers left Shockley and started Fairchild Semiconductors (stay with me here).

The "defection" led to the engineers being called the "Traitorous Eight." This was big news. But the bigger news is that two of the eight went on to start a company named Intel.

Intel dominated the semiconductor industry and has been the brains of billions of computers around the world for more than fifty years. There is a high probability that the tech company where you are interviewing is built on Intel's technology.

Knowing the origin story of the <u>industry</u> will make you much more interesting when interviewing. Of course, go to the company's website and read some bios about the people you would work with like all the quick and dirty thinkers will do, but do more.

Why not do the extra work and splurge for the $19 to run full background checks on a few people at the company? There are plenty of firms out there that can tell you with a click of a mouse:

- Marital and family status
- Delinquent payments
- Fines and judgements
- Arrest records

And many more interesting facts, especially if you're the nosy type.

Hey, the company is going to put you through the ringer of testing and background and reference checks. Why not do the same to them?

Another avenue to pursue is studying, not browsing, the employment history of potential bosses and co-workers. Take your searches deep.

For starters:

- View a potential boss's profile on LinkedIn.
- Stalk him on Facebook and other social media.
- Gather the list of <u>his</u> previous employers.
- Go to the websites and do searches on the previous employers.
- Go deeper on any lawsuits, controversies, and anything newsworthy about those previous companies. Was he involved in any of this?

In doing these deeper searches, we are trying to uncover information that people will not readily share. If you were a vice president and had your own parking space and a corner office, would you want sexual harassment allegations filed against you ten years ago to be a topic of conversation with an interviewee?

Have enough information so you can ask the interviewer about **her** past employment and experiences and what she learned from it all. Turn the tables.

How you prepare for any high-stakes interview is a Tectonic Decision and should be treated as such.

Chapter 24: Titan's Catastrophic Implosion Caused by Investors?

On June 18, 2023, the Titan submersible was on a voyage to 12,500 feet below the sea to visit the remains of the Titanic, which hit an iceberg and sunk off the coast of Newfoundland in 1912. More than 1,500 people lost their lives on the Titanic.

Titan's pilot was Stockton Rush, CEO of OceanGate Technologies, which built and owned Titan. Rush and four passengers climbed into the sub and Titan's hatch was bolted shut from the outside. Once secured, Titan slid into the forty-five-degree waters of the North Atlantic Ocean. A short time later, Titan imploded, killing all aboard.

My theory of how the Titan disaster unfolded is centered around money.

To gain perspective on the costs of deep-sea exploration, let's look at an unrelated company in the industry called Triton Submarines. Based in Florida, Triton makes submersibles like Titan. The Triton product line starts with one-man submersibles that are classified to about 1,000 feet of depth and cost about $3 million. A cool toy for the owner of a large yacht. The top of the line is a three-person model classified to 36,000 feet, outfitted for scientific exploration, and costs about $40 million. These numbers do not include the expense of support ships, permits, fuel, crew, and many other costly items required for successful missions. Deep-sea exploration is an expensive business.

By all accounts, Stockton Rush was a wealthy man from a wealthy family. But was he wealthy enough to fund the entire build and operation of a five-person submersible that could go to the depths of the Titanic? I don't think so.

Records indicate that OceanGate raised $19 million of investment during its fourteen years of existence with almost all of it in a 2020 round of funding. This seems like a paltry sum when we look at the personal funds spent by other modern-day explorers like space-tourism company Blue Origin, into which Amazon's Jeff Bezos has poured more than $7 billion. Further, records indicate the $19 million came from twenty-two investors. While $860,000 per investor is nothing to sneeze at, in the world of private equity and venture capital, this was a mom-and-pop, friends and family pool of capital.

If we go back to the chapter on moonshots, there was a key takeaway: Elon Musk (SpaceX) and George Lucas (LucasFilms and *Star Wars*) maintained full control of their enterprises since they funded all the early, high-risk phases of the businesses with their own money.

When Rush needed money, he didn't have a Bezos-sized bank account, so he took on investors and then had a completely different and new level of accountability. He needed to deliver results so his investors could eventually get a return on their money. No more exploring for the sake of science and humanity. It was more about producing spreadsheets, reporting progress, and delivering on promises made to his investors.

There are about ten submersibles in the world that are classified to dive to the depths of the Titanic. A submersible or "sub" is different from a submarine in that a submersible must be launched from a support ship and hoisted in and out of the water. A sub is "classed" by an outside agency to certify its integrity to a certain depth, particular type of operation, and compliance with international standards and maritime laws, among other things. The classification process is like the inspections that are done when you are building a home or doing a renovation. At each step of the way, different specialists verify components of the build. The electrical team checks out the wiring on the sub while the materials team tests the hull for integrity under pressure and so on. Classifications slow down the time for a sub to get to market and increase the costs of the build.

Rush and team wanted none of this and skipped the entire classification process. In industry parlance, Titan was an "unclassed vessel" and the only such vessel seeking to go to Titanic depths.

After a few years of trial and error, OceanGate raised its January 2020 round of funding.

> OceanGate will take advantage of lessons learned during the construction of its carbon-hulled Titan submersible, which was originally built for Titanic journeys. Rush said tests that were conducted at the Deep Ocean Test Facility in Annapolis, MD., revealed that the Titan's hull "showed signs of cyclic fatigue." As a result, the hull's depth rating was reduced [by OceanGate] to 3,000 meters [9,842 feet].

> "Not enough to get to the Titanic," Rush said.

> Source: OceanGate raises $18M to build a bigger submersible fleet and set up Titanic trips, Alan Boyle, GeekWire, January 9, 2020

So, we have a situation where it looks like OceanGate's original carbon-fiber hull was not holding up, was never classified by a maritime agency, and the company was running out of money.

What could go wrong?

The one investor presentation I would love to see is the one from the January 2020 funding.

What promises and projections did OceanGate have to make to entice investors to fund the deal?

Since the company was already taking customers on dives, and just not to Titanic depths, this felt like a round of funding to refine the product and move into the big time by offering Titanic visits. It did not have the feel of a round of research and development funding, in which the company would come back with a prototype or test vehicle in a few years.

In essence, after accepting the 2020 funding, the company was now under the gun to deliver those Titanic trips, one way or another. This is where quick and dirty thinking sealed the fate of OceanGate, Rush, and the four passengers on Titan.

In speaking with reporter David Pogue, who went on a previous Titan voyage, Rush said, "At some point, safety is just a pure waste." Surely these remarks are taken somewhat out of context, but it does indicate the attitude OceanGate had regarding safety.

After his trip, Pogue commented to a *USA Today* reporter: "Some of the ballasts are old, rusty construction pipes. There were certain things that looked like cut corners."

Rush's competitors and colleagues pleaded with him to slow down and have his new design classified because there had not been a commercial submersible fatality in more than sixty years; and what was bad for OceanGate would be bad for the industry.

This is not after-the-fact CYA.

There is a letter to Rush signed by a few dozen members of the Marine Technology Society, the industry group for submersibles, imploring Rush to have his design classified. This letter was written in 2018, five years before the catastrophe and around the time that OceanGate realized its then-current design would not hold up to Titanic depths and needed to raise more money.

Rush's response to these criticisms was that he was doing something new and different and classification agencies and unnecessary safety standards only slowed things down. He did, however, stop using phrases like "Titan meets or exceeds classification standards from DNV." (DNV is one of the lead classification organizations.)

He also boasted that Titan was designed in conjunction with NASA and the University of Washington. Neither organization confirmed any involvement with OceanGate beyond OceanGate's purchase of excess carbon fiber from NASA.

This brings us back to the question of why was he in such a hurry and why all the hype when dealing with a device that put his and others' lives at risk? Was it pressure to deliver for those pesky investors?

After its original carbon-fiber hull design showed signs of weakening at less-than-Titanic depths, OceanGate raised its big round of funding but stayed with carbon-fiber as the hull material.

A word about carbon fiber:

Carbon fiber is the ultimate high-strength lightweight material and is used in the construction of automobile frames, aircraft parts, and a variety of sports equipment like bicycles, canoes, tennis racquets, helmets, and golf clubs. It is truly a miracle of modern engineering, but it has never really been tested as a material to withstand the crushing pressure that occurs at Titanic depths.

Carbon fiber also brings down the overall cost of building and operating a submersible. All the other deep-water subs are made of much heavier steel and/or titanium and are constructed as spheres since the combination of materials and shape provide the greatest ability to withstand the pressure created by thousands of feet of ocean depth.

But such a design is not ideal for tourism. The OceanGate design was cylindrical and was like sitting in the fuselage of a small passenger plane, complete with a toilet, and could fit five passengers. The lighter weight of Titan also kept costs down since it did not require the bigger hosting ships with more sophisticated lifting mechanisms that were needed by the titanium vessels. (In fact, the hosting ship actually towed Titan in the water to the destination, which was unusual since most submersibles sit atop the deck on the ship and are hoisted up and down out of the water.)

After the funding, OceanGate went ahead with its updated carbon-fiber hull and aggressive schedule to get to Titanic depths. Previous passengers on Titan mentioned how Rush was proud that he was using a re-purposed gaming console for control of the sub. Versions of gaming consoles are used on some U.S. Navy ships and submarines, but only for specific functions. There were no standard communications with the surface, but text messages were used instead. There were few redundancies in Titan's systems and on a prior voyage, passengers were instructed to rock back and forth to help the sub drop its weights so it could re-surface.

Rush portrayed himself as a maverick who dared to do things differently. His lifetime record of achievements includes becoming a professional pilot at nineteen years old and modifying an existing small submersible and successfully diving in it. He also was involved in a handful of miscellaneous ventures. His record is not without accomplishment, but does it justify the level of faith that people had in him?

Another troubling data point is that as Titan was being constructed, OceanGate's chief pilot, David Lochridge, raised his concerns about Titan's design and materials to OceanGate's senior management. Lochridge wanted the vessel to get classified. OceanGate did not want to spend the time or the money. Lochridge was terminated for "leaking confidential information." Lochridge was the anti-quick-and-dirty thinker.

In addition to not going through the classification process, Titan's hull did not undergo "Non-Destructive Testing," or NDT. NDT is an important branch of materials science and is exactly what it sounds like. In a destructive test, the material is stressed to the point that it breaks down. For example, a flame could be held up to the titanium hull of a submersible to test the temperature at which the material in the hull breaks down.

For obvious reasons, NDT is the preferred approach for industrial projects like Titan. NDT utilizes x-rays, sonar, and other methods to look inside the material to test its molecular structure and look for structural defects in real time. NDT could have followed the impact of multiple dives of the Titan to identify structural changes and defects before they became catastrophic or life-threatening.

"I was stunned to learn that the Titan submersible had supposedly not undergone any NDT testing," said Greg Weaver, president of WeaverNDT, and an NDT professional with nearly twenty-five years of experience.

Source: "Alleged Lack of NDT on Titan Submersible 'Stuns' Many in Industry," Quality Magazine, July 10, 2023.

NDT professionals acknowledge that the NDT process would not have guaranteed a different outcome for Titan, but nevertheless, were puzzled as to why such testing was not done.

Finally, there is the unexplored relationship between OceanGate's founders. Together with Rush, OceanGate was founded in 2009 with Guillermo Söhnlein. Söhnlein left OceanGate in 2013 but retained his ownership stake. What did he do when he left? He started Blue Marble Exploration.

Blue Marble's website features a picture of a scuba diver in the ocean with the words, "We're on our way to explore the rest." The next Blue Marble trip in a sophisticated submersible is to Dean's Blue Hole, an essentially uncharted deep-water destination in the Caribbean.

Do you think this was an amicable split with Rush? I don't.

While Söhnlein has spoken out in the media in defense of Rush and OceanGate after the Titan disaster, what other move did he have? Anything other than a staunch defense of his former partner would have created a story of its own that Söhnlein probably did not want circulating.

From the Blue Marble website:

An entrepreneur with a passion for exploration, Guillermo Söhnlein has successfully launched ten for-profit ventures and four nonprofit organizations focused on technology innovation, space commercialization, and ocean exploration. An expedition leader, submersible pilot, and scuba diver, as co-founder and CEO of OceanGate (2009-2013), Söhnlein led six ocean exploration expeditions with crewed submersibles in Puget Sound, Monterey, Catalina Island and Miami.

So, was Söhnlein the original CEO of OceanGate and then Rush took over after Söhnlein left to start a directly competitive company? Surely Söhnlein had plenty of time to update the Blue Marble website if the "CEO" part of OceanGate were not true. At a minimum, there appears to have been a major difference of opinion between the founders.

The financial/business timeline leading up to the implosion is an interesting one.

2013: Founders part ways
2013: One founder starts a direct competitor
2016: Chief Pilot wants Titan classified
2018: Chief Pilot fired
2018: Industry pleads for Titan classification
2020: $19 million raised from twenty-two investors

Before its ill-fated journey in June 2023, Titan made two successful voyages to Titanic in 2021 and 2022. But the industry's concerns about the "delamination" or breaking down of the carbon-fiber hull were only exacerbated with each dive. When the Titan wreckage was found 12,500 feet below the surface and about a quarter of a mile from Titanic, the carbon-fiber fuselage had imploded because of the enormous pressure at depth. (An implosion happens when something collapses upon itself. Think of crushing a paper cup between your hands.) Remaining intact were the two end cones of the sub.

Both were constructed not of carbon fiber, but of titanium.

We do not yet know the full story of OceanGate and Titan. Investigations may not be completed until late 2024 or sometime in 2025. But the facts support a quick and dirty approach taken by OceanGate when compared with basic industry safety standards, as well as common sense. Additionally, OceanGate registered its vessels outside the U.S., allowing it to skirt the additional slowdowns and costs of the U.S. legal system.

When viewing the totality of the shortcuts and quick fixes used by OceanGate, it's easy to understand how the title of Ben Taub's excellent article in *The New Yorker* in 2023 says it all about Titan, "An Accident Waiting to Happen."

Chapter 25: Avoiding the Stupidity of Quick and Dirty Thinking

Remember those kids who were the smartest in the class as you grew up? Well, they still think they are the smartest and one of their tricks is heuristics.

Hey, I found a shortcut or rule of thumb those ordinary thinkers couldn't figure out.

This only metastasizes the heuristic problem into something worse. Those smart people are now in positions like Bossman or the OceanGate investors and want fast answers and results.

Don't get maneuvered into agreeing with the quick and dirty answer provided by a heuristic. If you do, you are sliding into the swamp of stupidity. Stop the conversation and hold the other participants accountable.

I don't care that three of the first six customers liked the product enhancement, it does not justify the multi-million-dollar investment to roll it out to the other 1,000 customers.

Don't fall into the trap of going through the motions in a high-stakes interview. Make yourself interesting. Avoid standard questions that every interviewee will ask. Do your homework well in advance. Know everything about the people you will be seeing and spend the time to learn the industry. Why not spend six or eight hours researching the company and its people if you may end up being hired and spending many years there? Maybe you can teach your interviewer something he or she did not know.

Being a boring and predictable interviewee who takes no chances with answers is a straight line into a stupidity trap.

Knowledge is power. Before going into an interview, get some knowledge, get some power, calculate your approach, and avoid stupidity.

As a college student looking for my first job after my upcoming graduation, I researched the company I wanted to work for, talked to current and former employees and industry competitors, and found out everything I could about the business. I went through several days of brutal interviews and a battery of exams administered by an outside psychological testing company. I was asked to come into the office for a meeting with the big guys. I could not have been more excited.

The meeting started out well. "We like you and want to offer you the job." The compensation was more than I could have imagined, and the company's brand was stellar. I was on my way.

As we were wrapping up (I tried not to talk once they said, "you're hired") there were some closing comments.

"We want to discuss a few things with you." Wow, were they going to make me a vice president or something right away?

The big guys proceeded to tell me that for my first year or two, I would not be working on any cool stuff, just following people, helping them, and learning on the job. In other words, I was going to be getting coffee for meetings and not participating in any high-level strategy discussions.

What? Was I being asked to be stupid?

I was crushed and, a week later, turned down the formal job offer. It's unfortunate that the last data point collected in my anti-quick-and-dirty-approach led to my decision: the job was not a fit. I did not realize it then, but this was one of my first Tectonic Decisions.

On a larger scale, don't become a trailblazer in an industry that puts people's lives at risk. OceanGate's refusal to get Titan classed or even run through basic materials testing is a cautionary tale. If you want to break new ground, quick and dirty does not work in an industry with a rigid safety framework and where lives are at risk.

Be like weight-loss champ Bradford and four-minute-miler Bannister and less like the hundreds of thousands of people who lined up for their Sensa refunds. Creating real solutions to problems is much different than getting the quick fix.

Section 7: Neglecting to Measure Twice

Among mortals, second thoughts are wisest.
~ Euripides

The saying "measure twice, cut once" is a rule for woodworking that is meant to avoid mistakes and waste, but it is really a warning for any serious decision-making to double check everything before making a commitment. We have all heard the advice, "You should think twice about that." But how often do we actually do so?

There are few classes of Tectonic Decisions that remain unexplored territory. Take the example of buying a car: You love it, your spouse loves it, and you can't wait to drive it off the lot. You knocked $500 off the sticker price and feel great. But you only measured once. The second measurement would be to scour the online car databases like Edmunds.com and triangulate in on what the **data say** is a good price. Keep going and read the reviews on the car to make sure it's not going to be in the shop every month.

None of this is new or radical thinking. But it is still amazing how often people, including influential decision-makers, do not use the car-buying example when signing off on a big investment or acquisition. There exist entire industries dedicated to due diligence and investigative work.

Why are so many smart people not smart enough to realize what they don't know? Probably because they want to be known as the "smartest" or the "fastest" to make a judgement. Many times, they are correct, but situations in which there is no second measurement are problematic since these constructs entail **Iceberg Risk**. As we know, 90 percent of an iceberg is underwater and not visible. Learn to identify situations that look great on the surface but do not hold up to that second measurement, since this is where your dreams will likely hit that iceberg.

Chapter 26: Can I Be Frank?

By most measures, JP Morgan (JPM) is the largest financial institution in the world. It has more than 250,000 employees and does business in almost every country on the planet. JPM has successfully acquired and assimilated multi-billion acquisitions like Chase Bank and Bear Stearns, but it is the relatively small acquisition of Frank Financial Aid that is instructive to examine.

Frank was built upon the fact that more than 85 percent of college-bound students apply for financial aid using the Free Application for Federal Student Aid (FAFSA).

I'm sure you have heard of it.

The problem Frank attacked was the mind-numbing complexity of filling out the FAFSA correctly. Many say they would rather fill out tax returns than work on the FAFSA. It is the cornerstone document used by federal and state agencies that award grants and loans, as well as the document used by two-year, four-year, vocational, and any other college to assign aid. The average total awards driven by the FAFSA are more than $20,000 per student. Real money.

Frank's basic service was free, and it helped users fill out the FAFSA, like popular tax preparation software like TurboTax. It offered various levels of paid consulting services to help applicants maximize the value of awards.

For JPM, the rationale for the acquisition of Frank was that it provided JPM greater reach into the population of college-bound young adults. By acquiring this client base, JPM would have the opportunity to penetrate this Generation Z population and have them start using JPM's credit cards, bank accounts, stock-trading functions, auto loans, home mortgages, and more. It seemed to make a lot of sense at the strategic level for JPM.

Prior to any acquisition being finalized, there is a period of due diligence, essentially an investigation by the buyer (JPM) of the seller (Frank) in this case. Rather than simply believing whatever the seller says, the due diligence process provides the buyer with the opportunity to review detailed information that supports the seller's claims.

Having been part of many due diligence processes myself as a buyer and as a seller, I can attest to the simple dynamic that exists in every diligence project: the seller wants to share as little as possible, and the buyer wants to know everything possible. This dynamic exists for the simple reason that once serious diligence starts, the buyer and seller have already agreed on price and other key terms (e.g., who gets employment contracts).

So, for the seller (like Frank), diligence is all downside. Think about when houses are bought and sold. A price is agreed on and then the buyer sends in the inspectors and comes back to the seller and says, "When we made our offer, we didn't know that the heat does not work in the upstairs bathroom. It will cost us $25,000 to fix it, so let's reduce the price by $25,000." In this case, the house buyer did her diligence and measured twice before cutting once.

In the case of Frank, JPM thought it was acquiring a profitable business with 4.2 million new accounts as targets for the menu of JPM services. These accounts were listed in a database and included name, address, and other personal information on each account. After the acquisition closed and $175 million changed hands, JPM discovered a disturbing fact about those 4.2 million accounts: more than 90 percent of them were fabricated.

Oops.

Soon after the merger closed, the bank took its shot and sprayed a portion of Frank's customer list with solicitations. Of 400,000 outbound emails, only 28 percent arrived successfully in an inbox, compared with the usual 99 percent delivery rate. Moreover, just 103 recipients clicked a link to Frank's website. It was, as the bank put it in its legal filing, "disastrous."

Source: How Charlie Javice Got JP Morgan to Pay $175 million for...What exactly? Ron Lieber, *The New York Times,* January 21, 2023.

As the JPM-Frank drama unfolded, we learned that the Frank CEO and *Forbes* 30-under-30-star Charlie Javice went to extraordinary measures to perpetrate the fraud at Frank. Javice hired a data sciences professor to create the fake accounts. She paid the professor $18,000 to generate the data.

The question is: Prior to the deal closing, did JPM measure anything? Frank was only in existence for a few years at the time of the JPM deal. There are about 1.6 million college applicants per year, so if Frank had 4.2 million accounts, it would have meant that almost every college applicant since Frank was founded was using Frank's service. That should have been a threshold question at the onset of any diligence activities and asked before major deal terms were constructed.

Just as troubling is the lack of rigor in the JPM diligence process. When I have been involved in diligence of large databases like the 4.2 million accounts at Frank, the process was straightforward: hire a diligence team from a national consulting firm, have the statistician create a representative sample of the 4.2 million accounts, and hand the sample over to a call center or mailing house to verify the existence of the sample accounts. In this case, a one percent randomized sample would have been 42,000 accounts and maybe a couple of weeks of work for a professional call center to verify each one. If, for example, only 50 percent of the sample could be verified, then the acquisition process would come to a full stop to determine what the heck was going on and the question would be, "Are we really buying 4.2 million accounts?"

Fraud is always a difficult one to pin down. Fraud must be "willful and intentional." Hiring a professor to generate fake accounts? Well, that's fraud.

Many times, there is a delicate dance between the buyer and seller during negotiations and diligence in which the buyer does not want to come on too strong and scare away or drive the seller to a different buyer. This is common behavior, especially in a competitive bidding process.

It's stupid.

If your questions as a buyer are going to anger or upset the seller, then so be it. If the seller walks because of your approach, believe me, the deal would have fallen apart for some other reason soon enough.

Chapter 27: Unstable Genius: Jeff Skilling, Enron

Jeffrey K. Skilling grew up as the son of a sales manager at an industrial company in Pittsburgh. Skilling was a ferocious student and earned a full scholarship to Southern Methodist University. After college, he worked briefly before attending Harvard Business School to earn his MBA. At his business school admission interview, Skilling was asked if he was smart. He allegedly replied, "Yeah, I'm fucking smart."

Skilling graduated in the top five percent of his Harvard class and took a job at McKinsey & Company, the world's top consulting firm. He soon became the youngest partner in the history of McKinsey.

With this kind of lofty start, where could Skilling's ambitions take him?

While working at McKinsey, his biggest client was Enron. Enron was an old school oil and gas pipeline company based in Houston. Enron and its predecessor companies, some of which date their origins to the 1920s, was a true brick-and-mortar company. Lots of pipelines running for hundreds of miles, and trucks, heavy equipment, and all the other hardware and buildings necessary to transport oil and gas around the country. Enron was a traditional asset-heavy business in a large and essential industry.

When Enron became Skilling's biggest consulting client at McKinsey, we had a classic clash of the old and the new. Skilling had a record of over-achievement and pushing the envelope while Enron was a successful, but stodgy, business.

So, what happened?

Anybody familiar with the Enron story from the 1990s knows Skilling left McKinsey and eventually became the president of Enron. But before Skilling left McKinsey to join Enron, he insisted on a key condition for taking the job: Enron must adopt mark-to-market accounting for the new energy-trading operation that Skilling was to manage.

There can be speculation as to why Skilling insisted on this accounting treatment, but I believe he knew that he was entering a new market (energy trading) and was creating some of the rules along the way. Having his preferred accounting treatment in hand would make it easier for Skilling to deliver big earnings since there were no reliable comparable businesses to benchmark against. In other words, it would be difficult for investors, analysts, and journalists to measure what he was doing, never mind measuring twice.

Mark-to-market (MTM) accounting is a method of valuing assets and liabilities based on their current market value rather than their historical cost. This means that the value of an asset or liability is recorded on the balance sheet at its current market value rather than its original purchase price. The purpose of mark-to-market accounting is to provide an accurate picture of a company's financial position by reflecting current market conditions.

For example, in the case of investments, if an investment is purchased at $100 and is valued at $110 in the current market, the value of the investment would be recorded as $110 on the balance sheet under mark-to-market accounting.

With its fleet of machinery and pipelines, Enron had never had any need for MTM, since MTM is a measure used in the financial industry where stock and bond prices change every second AND such prices are **visible and verifiable to players in the market**. (Hang in there, this concept is important.)

Imagine the discussion inside of Enron:

Bossman: Man, you guys stink. Why didn't you hit the locker room before showing up in my office?

CoverallsGuy: Sorry, Boss, but oil and gas are dirty businesses.

Bossman: Well, anyway, this new guy Skilling is coming on board, and he is a heavy hitter.

CoverallsGuy: Great, we need somebody to help figure out the best truck delivery routes and how to get better maintenance deals on our equipment. He know much about transporting sludge? I think it's the next big opportunity for us.

Bossman: Listen here, you idiot. Skilling is not coming to Enron to hang out in the garage and talk about the trucks and holding tanks. He is bringing a new concept to Enron called Mark-to-Market accounting.

CoverallsGuy: Huh? My brother-in-law is an accountant, maybe he can help us.

Bossman: I have a better idea: Hey Siri, what is Mark-to-Market accounting?

Now we have an oil and gas company adding an energy-trading operation with accounting that is used in the financial services industry.

How the heck can outsiders measure twice? What should they be measuring?

MTM was a non-negotiable condition for Skilling to join Enron and was necessary for him to continue his rise. As we shall see, MTM being live for Skilling as he joined Enron was the cause of the collapse and bankruptcy of the company.

Let's pretend you run a small division of Merrill Lynch and you have one hundred shares each of a dozen different companies (e.g., Apple, Disney, etc.). At the end of each day when the market closes, you need to mark your portfolio to the market and report your numbers up the management chain. Pretty simple, as all you do is look up the closing prices of Apple, Disney, etc., multiply each by the one hundred shares owned, and add up the totals. That's marking to market.

What's the big deal?

For the Merrill Lynch manager, marking to market was easy since the prices of his assets were **visible and verifiable by others.**

At Enron, things were a bit more complicated. First, let's remember how it works in Corporate America. The more earnings your division or team produces, the bigger the bonuses at year end.

Enter Skilling, a super-achiever who now had the accounting treatment he wanted. You guessed it, earnings went through the roof.

For several years, Enron's stock price did nothing but rise. Enron was on all the lists of the world's most admired companies and best places to work. And why not? With skyrocketing earnings came skyrocketing bonuses and a skyrocketing stock price. Everybody was happy.

While Enron was riding high, some started to question its financial statements. Most of us know that an income statement includes revenues and expenses. Revenues less expenses equal income.

But there are two other components of the financial statements that professional financial analysts examine: (i) the balance sheet, which lists assets (buildings, equipment, cash on hand) and liabilities (loans and amounts due to others) and (ii) the statement of cashflows that acts as a kind of connector of the income statement and balance sheet.

Finally, somebody was starting to try to measure twice before investing in Enron.

Enron kept the focus on those incandescent income statements and those ever-rising earnings.

But as reporters and analysts probed the full set of financials, things were not adding up. Part of this was the perversion of mark-to-market accounting by Skilling and his team. There were tons of assets on the Enron books that were illiquid and not easily valued. Skilling and team simply applied their own valuation (permitted under MTM) and made sure it increased each quarter, thereby creating income, pushing the stock price higher, and increasing bonuses.

Further, there were all sorts of debt deals executed by Enron to pay for some of these assets and the debt deals were not included in the financial statements. In other words, Skilling and team were making unorthodox investments that made the income statement shine, moved the stock price up, but burned a lot of cash.

Along the way, nobody doubted Skilling's brilliance. Yes, he was "fucking smart," no doubt. But he was also a heavy drinker and about as arrogant as they come. On an investor conference call with dozens of participants, Skilling did not like the question from an investment analyst.

What did he do?

He called the analyst an "asshole." After becoming the president of Enron, he suddenly quit, citing family reasons. Skilling subsequently sold tens of millions of dollars of Enron stock and the company collapsed less than 120 days after his resignation. And he testified (unsuccessfully) that he knew nothing of the company's problems when he resigned.

Skilling tried to turn a traditional industrial company into a trading and finance business. It turned out to be an accounting mirage that was impenetrable to interpretation and measurement by outside parties, until those parties started asking the right questions. Enron was liquidated through bankruptcy, its stock price went to $0, thousands lost their jobs, and millions lost their investments in Enron.

Skilling wound up serving fourteen years in prison for his role in deceiving the public and costing investors billions of dollars.

Chapter 28: WeWork and WeBurn Cash

Imagine a company that operated in 120 countries, 900 cities, and had 3,000 separate locations. Each location is a co-working or shared office space where you have your own cubicle or office but share common spaces and conference rooms with others. If there are ten co-workers on a floor, they may work at ten different companies. It would be interesting to meet and network with such a diverse group, especially if you are a solo entrepreneur or a startup with a handful of employees.

The information above describes a company called Regus. It was in business for more than twenty years before WeWork entered the market for shared office space in 2010. Regus is still in business and was several times the size of WeWork when WeWork imploded in 2019.

The WeWork story is also the Softbank story. While WeWork never heard of measuring twice, Japan-based Softbank, one of the largest venture investors in the world, certainly knew how to do it but, for whatever reason, did not exercise any caution with WeWork and lost a substantial portion of its more than $17 billion invested in the company.

WeWork started modestly with Adam Neumann as its co-founder and CEO. The "modestly" part did not last long. Neumann was a world champion spender of investors' money, promoter of what he saw as a new world order of people living together in harmony, and an expert at insider dealing for his own benefit.

What a guy!

To start, the WeWork business model was built on a faulty assumption. For example, WeWork would sign a ten- to twenty-year lease for three floors in an office building, creating a substantial liability for WeWork. It would increase that liability by making the capital investments required for the space to be useful for the one and two-person businesses that would sublease from WeWork. The problem was those subleases were for small pieces of the space and for short sublease terms (starting at one month).

If we build it, they will come.

WeWork promoted itself as a new age technology company and, unbelievably, was able to raise billions of dollars based on technology-company-like valuations. WeWork claimed it was not just a real estate company like Regus, but a whole different business model. In fact, nice sofas and fresh fruit in the water cooler was not a different model, but simply lipstick on a boring, but steady and proven real estate model.

We won't go into the Neumann eccentricities and profligate spending – traveling with his surfing coach, chartering Gulfstream jets like the rest of us ride the subway, and many other documented excesses -- but rather focus on how Softbank and other investors continued to pour money into WeWork at an astonishing rate even though the ability to measure twice was readily available to them. Prior to its failed IPO in 2019, it has been estimated that WeWork was burning an eye-watering $150 to $200 million in cash per **month**.

Before the failed IPO, investors, including Softbank, had access to all this information. They could see that WeWork's locations doubled in the past year to more than 500. Losses more than doubled. There was no sighting of a sustainable business model. Many times, with multi-location businesses like retail stores or WeWork, management rolls out a "same store" analysis, which is a legitimate financial exercise. What you would expect to see from WeWork in such an analysis would be something like, "For our locations open for at least thirty-six months, here are the profits we are making, so hang in there. Let us keep getting bigger since once locations are running for thirty-six months, we kick ass."

No such data were available from WeWork, yet Softbank stepped up to invest. And not just any investment: Softbank invested a total of $17 billion of debt and equity in WeWork. Did Softbank ignore the warning signs as WeWork was pitching it for investment dollars? Maybe, but this looks like a situation where Softbank wanted to use WeWork to make a statement about how big and bad Softbank was. The problem was that most of Softbank's other investments were software and technology focused. The beauty of a software company is operating leverage.

Operating leverage is simple to understand. Think of it as the hit song analogy. When a recording artist creates a song, there may have been thousands of hours of work and millions of dollars to get that song to the point where that first purchase or download of the song can happen. What is the cost for the second download, or the millionth download? Practically zero. The software business works in a similar way. Think about a popular tool like Microsoft Excel. Once it's in production, there are few costs other than hosting servers for users to pay and download copies.

Not so with an asset-intensive real estate business, that did not even own the real estate, but leased it. Most of Softbank's previous success was built around the operating leverage it witnessed at many of its portfolio companies. There was no leverage at WeWork. Each location needed desks, managers, water coolers, etc., so, it was no different than going back into the studio to try to make that second hit song. Softbank may not have fully understood the ordinary nature of the WeWork business and was dazzled by Neumann's talk of tech-enablement and a bunch of other new age chatter.

Or was Softbank stuck, and this just another classic case of collective denial? It was already deep into WeWork and may have been at the point where if it pulled its ongoing support, so would other investors and WeWork would collapse. Softbank never did that second measurement early in the life of its investment and continued to compound the error, rather than taking its medicine by eating the WeWork loss early and moving on.

Afterword

In August 2022, Neumann secured $350 million of funding from renowned venture capitalists Andreessen Horowitz, the largest check ever written by the investment firm. The funding was for Flow, Neumann's new venture that has been vaguely described as a WeWork for residential space. The venture firm says Flow will be, "community-driven, experience-centric service with the latest technology." Um, okay. More than a year after the announcement, Flow has yet to announce any deals or products.

In July 2023, Adam Neumann's family office, aptly named after the famous Portugal surf break Nazare Management, defaulted on a $31 million office building loan in San Jose, CA.

Seems like a paltry sum for such an alleged highflyer, don't you think?

In August 2023, WeWork said the following in a filing with the SEC, "Substantial doubt exists about the company's ability to continue as a going concern." WeWork filed for Chapter 11 bankruptcy protection on November 6, 2023.

As for Softbank, in August 2023, it sued a company called IRL for $150 million. IRL's primary service was a messaging application like WhatsApp. IRL was a Softbank portfolio company and 95 percent of its users were fake. Softbank, an allegedly sophisticated investor said it "relied on representations of management" in making its investment.

Sounds like a formula for stupid.

After the IRL fiasco was made public, other venture investors spoke out about the need to do more "uncomfortable" diligence on target companies, which to me means measuring twice and in some cases, measuring three or four times.

The $150 million lost investment in IRL is one thing, but Softbank has another trophy on the wall from its $1 billion failed investment in Wirecard, the German payment processor. Before its ultimate collapse, which included a middle-of-the-night private-jet escape to whereabouts unknown by COO Jan Marsalek, it came to light that Wirecard falsified records and forged transactions to induce the Softbank investment. Marsalek remains a fugitive and is speculated to be in Russia.

Chapter 29: Sex and Danger: Gawker

Gawker was a blog founded by Nick Denton in 2002. Denton was a former reporter for the *Financial Times* and Gawker was focused on celebrities, media, and anything else that could generate page views. Gawker brought us many critical things, such as:

- The Gawker Stalker let you add the location to an interactive map anytime you spotted a celebrity.

- A reporter who ate mozzarella sticks all day at a TGI Friday's to test the claim of endless appetizers.

- A high-profile CFO who paid $2,500 for a night with a gay prostitute.

You get the idea. Information that we just can't live without. And yet, Gawker was generating more than 20 million page views per month and was one of the most popular destinations on the web. Gawker ran close to the edge. Many of its stories were put up and then taken down when evidence emerged that the story was less than truthful. There was no balanced story writing at Gawker; it was all about sensationalism and page views.

Not a whole lot of measuring going on.

One of Gawker's biggest scoops was its publication of a sex tape of a guy named Terry Bollea. Bollea was recently divorced, and his good friend, Bubba (not a pseudonym), had invited him to have sex with his wife. When Bollea had asked him flat out if it would be taped, Bubba had said "no." Well, it was taped anyway, but Bubba left the tape in his desk. The story is only getting started at this point.

Bubba was a DJ. When a rival DJ allegedly broke into Bubba's office, among other things, he unwittingly stole the tape. The rival DJ just wanted to embarrass Bubba, so the Bollea tape was leaked, and Gawker had a big hit with its publishing. You may have never heard of Terry Bollea, but you may know him by his stage name, Hulk Hogan.

For decades, Hogan was one of the most recognizable names and faces in the world. As a six-foot seven-inch professional wrestler with a massive set of muscles and long blond hair, he was one of a kind. (I never met Hogan, but I did need to shoo him off the hood of my car once as he was leaning on it in the valet area of a hotel.) Hogan sued Gawker for invasion of privacy in 2016.

Going to trial is an expensive undertaking, especially in a situation in which Hogan sued Gawker for millions of dollars. Gawker and its insurers would fight back with a vengeance, since if it couldn't keep publishing whatever it wanted and generating those page views, Gawker would not have much of a future.

Why measure twice when we have such a good thing going?

Hogan and his lawyers trampled Gawker in the trial and the jury awarded him $140 million.

But here is where the story takes yet another turn. Billionaire Peter Thiel is one of the most successful venture capitalists ever. His early successes included PayPal (together with Elon Musk), Facebook (early investor and still a board member), and Palantir (analyzes massive databases for the CIA and others).

Thiel was also a subject of a Gawker story about ten years before the Hogan lawsuit. The story, "Peter Thiel is totally gay, people" was factually correct but, in Thiel's mind, was it really news or was destroying or disrupting people's lives as a hobby for some?

Thiel was known to be gay to a small circle of his friends, but the Gawker story changed the dynamic. He was publicly outed in 2007, which was a different time than today.

We should note that over the past twenty years, research indicates that acceptance of same-sex marriage has become mainstream. In 2003, more than 60 percent of the U.S. population opposed gay marriage, while today, more than 60 percent now support it.

After the Hogan verdict was announced, it came to light that Thiel had funded Hogan's legal costs to the tune of approximately $10 million. Hogan settled with Gawker for something in the range of $30 million; but it was over for Gawker, which soon filed for bankruptcy and was eventually shut down. As for Denton, he filed for personal bankruptcy.

A simple lesson here: Gawker and Denton should have thought twice about outing someone as gay, the publishing of a sex tape of such a high-profile individual and how it could ruin lives, rather than rush it to publication to generate a week's worth of page views.

Chapter 30: Measuring Twice, Going Big: Starbucks

When we look at the table below, it would be rational to conclude that it is a good time to get into the coffee business in the U.S. if you believe in one critical assumption:

Coffee consumption per person in the U.S. will one day approach the consumption experienced in the top coffee-consuming countries.

Per-Capita Coffee Consumption (kg/year)

1.	Country	Consumption
2.	Finland	12.0
3.	Norway	9.9
4.	Iceland	9.0
5.	Denmark	8.7
6.	Netherlands	8.4
7.	Sweden	8.2
8.	Switzerland	7.9
9.	Belgium	6.8
10.	Luxembourg	6.5
10.	Canada	6.5
25.	United States	4.4

If we look back at the example of Webvan, the company cratered because it relied on a similar philosophy upon which to build its business model.

Webvan looked at the consumption of its services in the San Francisco Bay Area (the Webvan initial market) and extrapolated those results to new geographies. As we discussed earlier, other markets did not behave like the Bay Area and Webvan didn't make it.

Let's move back to our chart. Can we use the top-consuming countries as an aspirational goal, start a coffee business in the U.S., and expect U.S. consumption to converge toward the top markets and give us a successful business?

A company called Starbucks made this bet and was right. By the way, Starbucks was founded in 1971, the chart above includes data from 2016, after Starbuck's had already opened more than 10,000 stores in the U.S. during the prior fifteen years.

Part of the Starbucks lore is the story of when CEO Howard Schultz visited Milan, Italy, and observed the sheer volume of cafes and places to get coffee in the city. He thought about why such density is not yet present in the U.S., a simple observation (measuring once) he was easily able to verify with data (measuring twice).

As it turned out, Schultz was right, sort of. In the U.S., it was not so much a demand for coffee as it was for a place to hang out, drink coffee, and get work done. If you go into many Starbucks locations in the middle of a workday, you can see what they are really selling: meeting space.

Before Starbucks and other coffee shops took the U.S. by storm, coffee was boring and almost a chore. You purchased a tin can of ground coffee at the grocery store, poured it into a paper or aluminum filter, added water, and waited for the coffee to brew. Whew, but it was part of the daily ritual for tens of millions of Americans.

The genius behind Starbucks was translating to the U.S. the cultural significance of the European café as a gathering place. On top of that, Starbucks built a track record of innovation matched by few other businesses in modern history. Seemingly small things like writing the customer's name on the cup created the feeling of personalization and exclusivity. Suddenly, people were fine paying more for one cup of fancy coffee than they paid for an entire can of coffee grounds.

But Starbucks took innovations much farther and added merchandise, cold beverages, and food to its menu. In fiscal year 2022, only 60 percent of Starbucks sales were from beverages and a good portion of that from innovative cold beverages like Frappuccino.

Did we mention the record label? Starbucks started *Hear Music* and cut exclusive deals with artists like Ray Charles and Alanis Morrisette.

Starbucks was an early adopter of free Wi-Fi and internet service in its stores. I can remember several colleagues preferring to meet and work at Starbucks because the internet connection was better, and the mood and music were more relaxing than our office.

Starbucks pushed us to rethink our thinking about coffee. By importing the European model to the U.S., Starbucks reset the playing field. It was not about getting a good cup of coffee anymore; it was all about the coffee experience. But it all started because of some careful measurement and thinking at the origin of the decision-making.

Chapter 31: Avoiding the Stupidity of Not Measuring Twice

Of all the stupidities, this one is the most avoidable. When we see something we want to do like launching a new product, pursuing an acquisition, or setting bold goals, we justifiably get excited. When we are too high or too low emotionally, we tend not think at our best.

There is no intellectual shame in admitting that you are technically inexperienced in doing a transaction like the Frank acquisition. Why not access expert resources? This is not an advertisement to use consultants, but one for locating a trusted and objective third party to make sure you get that second measurement. It still confounds me that JP Morgan threw up such an airball on the Frank acquisition, until we dig a little deeper.

In the year prior to the Frank acquisition, JP Morgan's stock languished at about $100 per share. So, what did the company do? It went on an acquisition spree to excite its investments and energize its stock price. In the year of the Frank deal, JP Morgan did 45 acquisitions – more than any other year in its history. Its stock price increased to $175 per share as they were jamming in all those deals, including Frank. A year later, its stock price was back at $100 per share.

Believe it or not, investment bankers and consultants can be helpful. You don't have to hire them but let them pitch you for the business and then press them for insights into your proposed deal. In other words, gather data, gather data, gather data, then assimilate your thoughts before you decide you are all in on a Tectonic Decision.

All of this makes me wonder how Enron, WeWork, and Gawker got away with it for so long. These companies had plenty of experienced investors and board members. The problem is that as long as everybody is making money, why disrupt a good thing? WeWork was able to keep raising billions of dollars, Enron's stock price was rising, while Gawker was killing it on page views. To torture an old saying, in each of these situations, **something was broken, and nobody dared to fix it.**

Section 8: Putting It All Together

I try to encourage people to think for themselves,
to question standard assumptions....
Don't take assumptions for granted.
Begin by taking a skeptical attitude toward
anything that is conventional wisdom.
Make it justify itself. It usually can't.
Be willing to ask questions about what is taken
for granted. Try to think things through
for yourself.

~ Noam Chomsky

We have been through stories and examples of how people made good and bad decisions. In every case, the odds of a making a proper decision skyrocket if we avoid the seven deadly stupidities. Our impulsive, emotional thinking, which pulls us into the swamp of the stupidities, is constantly at war with our need to be logical and structured in our decision-making process. Awareness of this struggle is half the battle.

A friend of mine, Guy Kawasaki, reviewed an early draft of this book and asked, "Do you think more success stories should be discussed?" Now, Guy is not just any friend. He is the author of sixteen books, the original brand evangelist at Apple and Canva, and is currently one of the busiest guys I know. Look him up. You will learn something from his writings, podcasts, and talks.

At the time of Guy's question, I did have a handful of success stories in the draft, but there were so many examples of smart people getting trapped by stupidities, I stayed focused on cases like the Webvan investors who could not get out of their own way, or the captain of *El Faro*, who could have easily had a different outcome if not for the stupidities, and then the champion of those felled by the stupidities, former McKinsey chairman and convicted felon, Rajat Gupta.

But after writing a good piece of this book, I realized that there were some heroes out there who beat the stupidities and their stories should be told as well. We will first focus on the remarkable success story of a Soviet soldier who faced and slayed all seven deadly stupidities.

Chapter 32: Soviet General Petrov: The (Almost) End of the World

There is a book and movie from the 1960s called *Fail Safe*. It is the story of how a fleet of U.S. military aircraft mistakenly flies across the Atlantic to drop a nuclear bomb on Moscow.

The entire time the planes are in flight and the U.S. is trying to recall the mission, the leaders of both countries are on the phone with the U.S. telling the Soviets that this is a mistake and not an act of war. The U.S. bombers do not respond to the recall messages because they believe the messages are fake and sent by the Soviets.

The bomb was dropped, and Moscow was destroyed. The U.S. president offers a solution to avoid an all-out nuclear war with the Soviets: he will have a U.S. military aircraft drop a similar bomb on New York City. In the end, Moscow and New York are destroyed, but each country stays intact.

Crazy stuff, right? But this was the way it was back then.

Here is a transcription of part of the movie that gives us a sense of the feeling between the U.S. and the Soviet Union at the time. This is part of the dialogue where a professor is educating U.S. military leaders:

….The Russian aim is to dominate the world. They think that Communism must succeed…..

….These are Marxist fanatics, not normal people. They do not reason the way you reason, General Black. They're not motivated by human emotions such as rage and pity. They are calculating machines…..

So, imagine the real-life case of Soviet Colonel Stanislav Petrov.

In 1983, at the peak of the Cold War, Petrov was the officer on duty when the Soviet's early warning system indicated a launch of missiles from the U.S. was targeted at the Soviet Union. The system told him five missiles were inbound. The missiles, each with multiple nuclear warheads, would strike and detonate in the Soviet Union in less than twenty minutes.

The way the Soviet system worked at the time, if Petrov followed protocol and immediately reported the incoming missiles up the chain to the Soviet command, the automatic response would be a full-scale nuclear retaliatory strike on the U.S. The end of the world. Not cool.

But something was not quite right in Petrov's mind, so he hesitated to report the strike up the chain. He started to think deliberately, assemble data, and go full-on Kahneman System 2. Remember, his basis was U.S. vs Soviet Union, and it was winner-take-all.

Petrov thought, *Why just five missiles and not an all-out strike from the U.S. on the Soviet Union? Five missiles would be akin to the U.S. "poking the bear," and the Soviets would respond with overwhelming force.*

Strategically, the five-missile attack made no sense to Petrov. Warfare expert Jeffrey Lewis from an NPR interview:

> "[Petrov] just had this feeling in his gut that it wasn't right. It was five missiles. It didn't seem like enough. So even though by all of the protocols he had been trained to follow, he should absolutely have reported that up the chain of command and, you know, we should be talking about the great nuclear war of 1983, if any of us survived."

> Source: Stanislav Petrov, 'The Man Who Saved The World,' Dies At 77, Greg Myre, NPR, September 18, 2017.

What did Petrov do? Simple. Before making this monumental Tectonic Decision, he changed the dynamic of the decision-making process.

Petrov had his team verify the facts before a decision was made. As it turned out, there was a reflection from the sun off the clouds that the early-warning system interpreted as incoming missiles. Once verified, there was no need for Petrov to pull the trigger. He made the decision without his palms sweating and heart racing.

Given the tensions between the countries at that time, nobody would have faulted Petrov for following protocol and hitting the button. Petrov was heavily criticized and interrogated by the Soviets for his behavior. Years later, he was hailed as an international hero.

How Petrov Beat the Stupidities

He did not surrender to FOMO. Given the tensions between the U.S. and Soviet Union at the time, it would have been easy for Petrov jump right in, pull the trigger, and be in the middle of the action. Staying out of the action was much harder, but he managed to overcome his fear and think rationally.

He did not rely on family and friends. In this circumstance, Petrov could have accessed his comrades, both above and below him in rank, to solicit advice. Doing so may have created more problems for Petrov than he wanted since his "friends" may have turned him in for treason for even questioning the protocol. Remember in the family and friends chapter how we talked about how only one of the three outcomes was a good outcome when relying on advice from family and friends? Petrov's situation was no different, except the fate of the world rested upon his decision.

He did not use quick and dirty thinking. If he did, he would have said, "System says fire the missiles; let's fire first and ask questions later." Kudos to Petrov for avoiding this stupidity.

He was not blinded by the upside. Even if he was saving the world (for real), Petrov knew that in the Soviet military, there was no upside to his decision. He was not getting promoted for questioning protocol or hesitating like he did. He likely understood his decision was all downside for him personally. The glory and upside would have been in pressing the button and having the Soviet Union destroy the United States.

He did not go for a moonshot. Quite contrary to trying to change the world and revolutionize the Soviet defense infrastructure, Petrov did the opposite. He stayed focused on what incremental changes he could make to improve the situation like rechecking instruments and being satisfied that his data were verified. Another day at the office.

He did not trust the media. In the introductory paragraphs above, we see how the U.S. viewed the Soviets and how the Soviets viewed the U.S. These attitudes were only amplified by the media and Petrov, as a Soviet commander, was well-schooled in the perception of the U.S.

These are our enemies and must be destroyed.

Yet, he did not let the media dictate his emotions and take over his decision-making.

He did measure twice. Boy, did he ever. Perhaps the paltry five-missile attack did not make sense to Petrov at a subconscious level or maybe he said it out loud: "Why would they only send five missiles instead of five hundred?" In either case, Petrov measured once by registering the problem, then did the critical second measurement by rechecking the instruments to realize it was not unprovoked attack by a hated adversary, but a weather anomaly.

Quite a guy, this Petrov was.

What was the key to his clear-headed thinking? He did not try to add anything to the process but, rather, he deduced it would better to eliminate items from the decision-making.

Petrov knew he was on the cusp of a Tectonic Decision and whether he realized it, he clicked through each of the seven deadly stupidities and steered clear of them all.

We must be more like Petrov and move stupidities out of the way to clear a path to a better decision.

Who Are Our Stupidity-Defying Heroes?

Going back to our Boorstin definition of a hero in the chapters of Section 5, Petrov fits the description. He is known for his achievements and contributions. Done. But who are the other heroes that we have met that have defeated the stupidities?

Surely, Apple executive Gassée, who had the nerve to question the Theranos claims of a new world order in blood testing. Gassée was successful because he did not go for the assumptions. He wanted to see the data.

I think we must add young Tyler Shultz to our list of heroes as well. He risked his career to expose the untruths at Theranos that could have put millions of lives in jeopardy.

RationalMom gave TigerMom a beating and TigerMom still hasn't learned her lesson. Stay away from listening to TigerMom and others who are so sure of themselves that they exclude valuable input from others. Hang out with RationalMom.

And how can we not include Rosalie Bradford as a success after she lost 900 pounds? Deliberate thinking and not reaching for a quick and dirty answer. We would all be better off with thinking more like Bradford.

Some may disagree, but Peter Thiel is a hero to me for holding the media accountable. This is a lost art that has been overrun by the internet and a blog on every corner.

Elon "Moonshot" Musk? Well, you decide. But Musk, George Lucas, and others like them who put their reputations and own money behind their dreams have a special place in the universe of this writer. They are unlike portfolio-driven venture and private-equity investors that seek to "risk-manage" and spread dollars across dozens of bets hoping one or two will pay off. There is a lot of spreadsheets and MBA-speak from these "professional investors," but only occasional world-changing activity and minimal personal risk.

Finally, let's not forget about the true hero of this book: CubicleGuy. He taught us that its permissible to question authority if you have your facts and Bossman does not. I think this is the most important takeaway from this book: CubicleGuy is aware of the stupidities and knows how to avoid them.

We all should be so lucky.

Acknowledgements

This book is the accumulation of more than 30 years of in-the-field research. While I have always been interested in, and have read extensively about, the fields of cognitive psychology, organizational behavior, and decision-making, the way I have learned these lessons is from the School of Hard Knocks. First-hand experience with many decision-making scenarios, most with significant consequences, has given me the insight and motivation for this work.

As a new author, I needed somebody to teach me the rules and provide guidance for how this writing-a-book thing works. Without JD Kleinke pushing me through each step of the process, this book never would have happened. JD and I have been lifelong friends and collaborators and I need to publish another half dozen books to be in his league. Without JD, there would be no *Seven Deadly Stupidities* – he coined the title in one of our brainstorming sessions.

Although I had read all of Guy Kawasaki's books over the years, I had never met him until my daughter, EmilyAnne, brought me to lunch with Guy after a morning of surfing. To say Guy has been generous with his time and insight over the course of this project would be a significant understatement. Most know Guy as accomplished author, speaker, and somebody who defined the role of a brand evangelist. I am lucky to know Guy as all those things plus I also know him as a loving family man, unselfish mentor, a surfer, and somebody who is now dedicated to helping others achieve success, or Guy puts it, become remarkable.

John De Santis gave his input on the manuscript and has been a tolerant listener and provider of insight throughout this journey. Thanks to Mark Finucane for his review of an early draft and to my podcast partner, Milen Hayriyan for her contributions to the book and podcast. Jennifer Wilkov of *Your Book is Your Hook* provided invaluable counsel, as well as top-notch editing. Thanks to Dan Heneghan for his non-stop energy, optimism, and interest in making this book successful.

Summerlynd Nelson brought in the Gen Z perspective, which will probably be the only perspective that matters pretty soon.

Guy Sansone took a chance, hired me, and taught me the world of crisis management upon which much of the thinking in this book is based.

Thanks to Carl Schramm and Steve Renn for teaching a young math geek how to write and so much more.

Special thanks to Rick Scott, who always made time to provide valuable guidance throughout our relationship.

In addition to providing music for the podcast, Jimmy Lohrius has been a reluctant, but helpful critic. I am grateful to Seth and Mary Baker for their endless encouragement, support, and willingness to go above and beyond to help me in any way. My nephew, Christopher Pierorazio, a professional musician, has been my tutor in the world of sound engineering for the podcast.

My sister-in-law MaryJo was an early reader and provided much-needed encouragement throughout the process. My niece, Maddie Pillari, a rising star and editor at Harper-Collins, helped guide me through the publishing world with the patience of a saint. In-laws Agatha and Joe were a quiet presence with me every step of the way.

Andy and Helen Cappuccino have been die-hard fans of the project since inception and insist this is big-time piece of work. I guess we will find out soon enough.

Thanks to Thomas Sarubbi, Ph.D., whose advanced chemistry skills guided me through the world of carbon fiber.

Thanks must go to all my children, MarieSarah (+Chris), EmilyAnne, Andrew (+Adrienne), Matthew, and Michael for putting up with their father insisting they read a few pages and provide immediate feedback. Hey, I helped with enough homework over the years, why not throw me a bone?

And let's forget my mom, Carol, who developed my early interest in reading by dropping me at the public library in Queens, NY for hours at a time – when I was in second and third grade. (Yes, she would be arrested if she did that today.)

This book was written on several cross-country RV trips with me doing the writing and talking and my wife and chief editor Rosanna doing the driving while strengthening the good parts and nixing the bad parts as the book took shape. She is a rare combination of critic and supporter, and it may be cliché, but this book is hers as much as it is mine.

About the Author

George Pillari has appeared on CNN, and been quoted in the *Wall Street Journal*, *New York Times*, and *Washington Post*.

He is an author or co-author of 21 articles in such publications as the New England Journal of Medicine and the American Bankruptcy Institute Journal.

George was an EY Mid-Atlantic Healthcare Entrepreneur of the Year.

As an undergraduate, he co-founded a company with two professors at The Johns Hopkins University. The company grew to more than 1,000 employees, went public, and traded on the NASDAQ, and was eventually part of IBM's Watson Artificial Intelligence business.

He went on to work as a crisis manager at more than 100 companies and was an objective source of truth for a company's board, investors, and lenders.

In these high-leverage decision-making situations, Mr. Pillari identified the errors in judgment and poorly constructed decision-making models that were consistently present in businesses that were failing. He organized these failures into *The Seven Deadly Stupidities.*

George has a B.S. in Mathematical Sciences from the Whiting School of Engineering at The Johns Hopkins University.

Additional Resources

Stupid.Blog is based on this book and contains much new material since we just can't keep up with the examples of stupidity that we run across. You can sign up for our weekly mails.

Podcasts based on this material can be found on Spotify and Apple Podcasts. A visual podcast is available on YouTube. Search for "Seven Deadly Stupidities."

I can be contacted at gp@stupid.blog and will respond to your emails.

Praise for the Author

"The truth hurts, which is why so many investors and businesspeople prefer to tell each other big, bold, happy stories bound inevitably for very unhappy endings.

The Seven Deadly Stupidities is the business book no one dared write until now. It is a hard, candid look at the blind spots, wishful thinking, and outright nonsense that drive too many business plans, narrated with dozens of real-world examples and wry humor.

If this book were required reading in MBA school, billions in investment capital would be better allocated, and thousands of well-meaning people would be spared professional embarrassments if not outright career wipeouts."

~ JD Kleinke, Healthcare Industry Pioneer, Author, and Speaker

"With the benefit of hindsight, it's easy to write about decisions that leaders make when things go wrong. However, what's difficult is to have the situational awareness to know when one is in a similar position and about to make the same mistakes.

With a great talent for storytelling, George Pillari succinctly unpacks some well-known cases and provides the reader the tools to help one have perspective, apply sound reasoning and avoid the same mistakes.

When reading this book, don't be surprised if you start to squirm a little. His stories, while describing unique situations, cut to the core of universal experiences. Some struck so close to my own journey that I thought I might very well be a human tuning fork for the various 'stupidities' he describes.

Regardless of where you are on your life's journey, whether just starting out, on the crest of the wave, or looking back on a full life, George Pillari is a delight to read, has a fresh and fun perspective, and provides useful lessons that can be applied immediately to our daily challenges whether at work, at home or at play."

~John De Santis, Chairman ISACA, a global information security consortium with 170,000 members

"The Seven Deadly Stupidities is insightful, humorous, and likely to be required reading for both entrepreneurs, CEOs and consulting pros. Like the Proverbs, there are wisdom nuggets on every page as Pillari reveals how we can learn from our flawed decision-making habits."

~Dan Heneghan, CEO Roundtable Chairman, C12 Forums - Richmond, VA

"I'm so glad to have found this book while still in college. So many good lessons here that I will not have to learn the hard way."

~Summer Nelson, UCLA Student, Gen Z Social Media Influencer, Barstool Sports, TMZ

"George makes it simple, '80% of success is avoiding stupidity.' The case studies and lessons drive home the point that even smart people make bad decisions all the time."

~Guy Kawasaki, Chief evangelist of Canva and author of 16 books, including Think Remarkable

Made in the USA
Las Vegas, NV
04 September 2024

94700044R00134